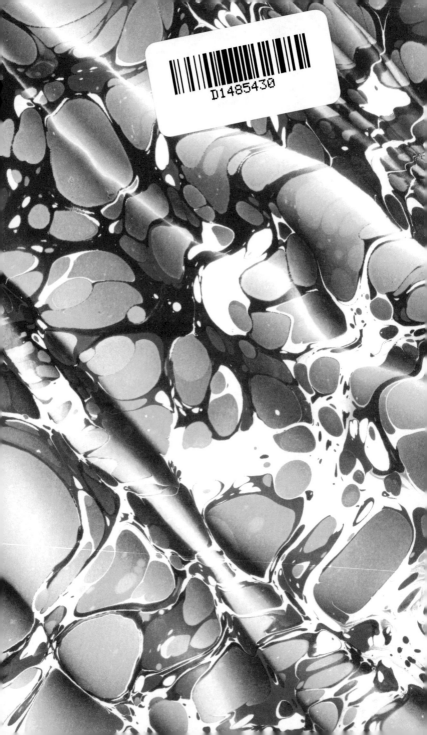

Dr Johnson's Reliquary of
Rediscovered
Words

Dr Johnson's Reliquary of
Rediscovered
Words

DR N. JOHNSON

■ SQUARE PEG

Published by Square Peg

2 4 6 8 10 9 7 5 3 1

Copyright © Neil Johnson 2008

First published by Marius Press 2008

Neil Johnson has asserted his right under the Copyright, Designs
and Patents Act 1988 to be identified as the author of this work

This edition published in Great Britain in 2009 by
Square Peg
Random House, 20 Vauxhall Bridge Road,
London SW1V 2SA

www.rbooks.co.uk

Addresses for companies within The Random House Group Limited can be found at:
www.randomhouse.co.uk/offices.htm

The Random House Group Limited Reg. No. 954009

A CIP catalogue record for this book
is available from the British Library

ISBN 9780224086387

Printed and bound in Great Britain by MPG Books, Bodmin, Cornwall

Contents

Acknowledgements

I take this opportunity to record my gratitude to my wife Susan, the rest of my family, and those of my friends (by no means all) who, after reading drafts of the Reliquary, did not immediately press me to seek expert medical advice or, at the very least, to take a holiday. I am particularly indebted to my publisher Rosemary Davidson of Square Peg for the enthusiastic encouragement she has given me in the development of this book, and to Anna Crone and Dinah Drazin for exercising their impressive creative flair – Anna's design for the cover is both striking and imaginative, whilst Dinah's skills in typography and layout give clarity and elegance to the book's pages. Special thanks are due to Tim Waller, my copy-editor, whose attention to detail, breadth of knowledge and general erudition have averted more than one solecism (where a comma persists before a defining relative clause it is at my behest and most certainly none of Tim's doing). And, of course, where would I have been without our wonderful politicians, bankers, educationalists, purveyors of 'fast food,' and those many others who all put in such tireless and sterling efforts to screw up the world?

Introduction

Words have an unfortunate way of getting lost. Some we simply forget; others we throw away and say good riddance to them; still others, it seems to me, lose themselves, diving for cover, as it were, from a world in which they no longer feel comfortable. Lost words – however they may have come to that state – may still be found again, by accident or by diligence, and, like old photographs rediscovered at the back of a drawer, may cause us to smile for a moment or two in remembrance of pleasures past.

That was the primary purpose of this little book when I first started work on it – to rummage about in the drawers of our language and pull out the words that the dear old thing had tucked away there, all warm and cosy, for safe keeping.

Alas for primary purposes! They seldom last very long – in my experience at least – and fall soon to secondary and even tertiary aims. It rapidly became clear to me that the drawers in which I had my hands were considerably more capacious than I had imagined possible, and that hiding within them were so many fugitive words that I would need to devote the rest of my lifetime, and a little more besides, to fishing them all out for closer inspection. I realized, in short, that my groping-about would need to have direction and purpose.

In the end, I decided to attend only to those words which I felt might still find a use in today's world, and to eschew those that owe their desuetude to the replacement of the technology of the cog, the thermionic valve or the logarithmic slide-rule by that of the silicon chip and other, stranger, inventions.

I also wished to say something about each word, in addition to providing a brief, formal definition, and this, together with the exigencies of time and of the format of the book I had in mind, has made my selection of words distinctly eclectic and personal.

The arrangement of the lexicon is simple. Immediately following each rediscovered word (and they are all – however unlikely in some cases it may seem – actual words, with none of them fabricated) I present a frankly idiosyncratic explanation of how the word is to be pronounced, and you will find a key to my phonetic system following this Introduction. There then follows a statement of the word's grammatical standing: i.e., whether it is a noun, adjective or verb, or whatnot. Next, I give a concise statement, in the words of today, of what the word used to mean (which may be, but is not necessarily, what it could, should or might possibly mean in its new life). Where a word once had several separate, though usually related, meanings (as most of them did), or even several different grammatical uses (as some of them did), I have selected just the one I think is most relevant to the word's revival.

Finally, I add a comment on the word. It may be an expansion, or possibly some form of illustration, of the formal definition, where I suggest that this may be retained. Elsewhere, it may be a suggestion for some new, richer, more vibrant role that I feel certain a reinvigorated and aspiring oldie could play to perfection. Sometimes I try to explain the origins or derivation of a word, and you will see that, in doing so, I have drawn on sources of information that you are unlikely to find referenced in other works of etymology (I have engaged in some pretty exhaustive research, I can tell you). Occasionally, my comments may be a bit ... well, *oblique* is probably the best way of putting it: I confess that more than an element of free association has crept in here and there. I can't help it, it's the way my mind works, and I'm afraid I have to leave it to you to figure out what I'm getting at.

I feel obliged to say something in explanation of the book's title. It is, of course, undoubtedly a *reliquary*, for the words are indeed relics – things that have survived from the past, are treasured for their past associations, and are to be treated with some degree of reverence. Naturally, it is my hope that, now they have been *rediscovered*, they may, with a bit of polishing-up and, where needed, given a fresh suit of clothes, yet again go forth to seek their fortune in a new and unfamiliar world. Of course, there may be pockets of linguistic resistance (the more remote, hillier parts of the country, perhaps, where woodsmoke still rises from the chimneys of stone-built hovels with floors of beaten earth) where some, even many, of the words listed in this book are still used on a daily basis, and where my suggested new uses for them would be greeted with derision. If so, I can offer only the excuse that such word-blessed places are unknown to me.

As will become clear, I have not attempted to dissociate my chosen rediscovered words from the hard facts of life; I have, in short, written as a realist. This reflects my deep feeling of responsibility for my protégées (not, you will note, protégés – for words, whatever the French may say to the contrary, as they usually do, are feminine, and must be accorded all the courtesies due to their sex). If I take it upon myself to push these shy, hitherto retiring (not to say retired) words out of the door to earn their living all by themselves, it surely behoves me to make sure that, at the very least, they go clear-sighted. I can, perforce, do no less for them than to tell them, straight from the shoulder, the way the world is, or at least the way I believe it to be.

Some readers will no doubt feel that my comments are less those of a realist than those of a reactionary or a cynic, and they may well be right (there's not a lot of difference between the three anyway). Others, I suppose, will detect the thickened toenails of age poking through the pages, and regard what I have written either as the distilled wisdom of many years' experience or, more likely, as clear evidence of arterial hardening coupled with a softening of the cerebral matter. Well, age may have few compensations, but not the least of them is not having to give a toss what anyone else thinks. So – realist, reactionary, cynic or old fool? Take your pick, but I'd prefer not to know what you think: my prejudices have taken years to perfect and hone, and I've become rather too attached to them to want to change them now.

Neil Johnson
Over Kellet, 2008

x

Pronunciation

I took the decision not to use the International Phonetic Alphabet to indicate correct pronunciation of the words presented in this lexicon, because, being used primarily by linguists, the phonetic symbols are not widely known amongst the general public. Instead, a simpler (though admittedly less precise) system has been used in which phonetic values are represented by letters, or combinations of letters, from the ordinary English alphabet. The syllables are separated by hyphens, and the stressed syllable is shown by underlining. For example, 'explanation' would be represented phonetically as: Ek-spla-nae-sh'n.

Phonetic symbols used

Symbol	As in	Symbol	As in
a	cat	ar	part
e	bet	air	hair
i	bit	ee	been
o	not	er	pert, shirt
u	cut	iy	bite
ae	late	oe	note

Symbol	As in	Symbol	As in
oo	c*oo*l	'	*uh* (barely
or	f*or*, sh*aw*l		pronounced)
oy	b*oi*l	b'l	tangi*ble*
ow	n*ow*, *ou*t	f'l	truf*fle*
*n	French *en, on*	g'l	wag*gle*
b	*b*at	j'n	dud*geon*
d	*d*og	k'l	cyni*cal*
f	*f*at	l'nt	indo*lent*
g	*g*ot	l'r	constabu*lary*
h	*h*at	l's	use*less*
j	*j*ug, nu*dge*	n's	bright*ness*
k	*c*at, ba*ck*	'nt	pursu*ant*
l	*l*ot	r'n	veter*an*
m	*m*an	r's	fib*rous*
n	*n*ot	's	abstemi*ous*
p	*p*at	s'r	ess*era*
r	*r*ip	sh'n	sta*tion*
s	*s*at, sen*s*e, fen*c*e	sh's	supersti*tious*
t	*t*op	s'm	lone*some*
v	*v*an	s'n	loo*sen*, li*sten*
w	*w*it	s'ns	efferve*scence*
y	*y*et	s'nt	efferve*scent*
z	*z*ap	t'l	bot*tle*
ch	*ch*urch	t's	anhis*tous*
dh	*th*at	v'l	gra*vel*
kh	lo*ch*	y'n	milli*on*
sh	*sh*irt	y'r	behavi*our*
th	*th*ink	z'm	schi*sm*
zh	sei*z*ure		

Note that there are only two peculiarities in my system that might cause any real grief. The first is my use of the bold italic *y* and **Y** to represent the consonant *y* as in 'yet.' This is to avoid any confusion with its use in compound vowel sounds, such as *oy* (as in 'b*oy*'), and *iy* (as in 'm*y*'). The second is the employment of a single apostrophe to indicate the barely pronounced *uh* sound in words like 'pretent*iou*s' (which I would present as: Pri-<u>ten</u>-sh's). The ultimate authority on the way particular words ought to be pronounced is, of course, the Oxford English Dictionary.

Grammatical Abbreviations

I have kept grammatical information to a minimum, and have used only a small number of abbreviations:

a   **Adjective**

adv   **Adverb**

excl   **Exclamation**

n   **Noun**: I have not distinguished formally between different classes of noun, such as those that are collective, common or proper, singular or plural, material (class), or abstract

vi   **Verb** (intransitive)

vt   **Verb** (transitive)

vi/vt **Verb** (used either intransitively or transitively, according to context)

Reliquary

A

Abacist. (<u>A</u>-ba-sist) **n**. *One who engages in numerical calculations*. May also be used (1) to mean someone whose mental activity does not depend upon a supply of electricity, or (2) in the more general sense of a person versed in any skill that is no longer taught in the UK.

Abator. (A-<u>bae</u>-t'r) **n**. *One who successfully deals with a nuisance*. A term which fell into disuse in the UK following the introduction of human rights legislation, and for which, unfortunately, there appears unlikely to be any great requirement in the foreseeable future.

Abdominous. (Ab-<u>do</u>-mi-n's) **a**. *Obese*. Most useful for describing the American lady who was sitting next to a passenger found unconscious and cyanosed at the end of a long-haul flight.

Ablatitious. (A-bla-<u>ti</u>-sh's) **a**. *Extractive; possessing the quality of taking something away.*

> *Though politicians offer much,*
> *With promises ambitious,*
> *They fund their generosity,*
> *By budgets ablatitious.*

Absonous. (<u>Ab</u>-so-n's) **a**. *Out of tune*. As applied to that particular kind of opera at the end of which some members of the audience are heard to remark loudly that it was even better than the last three times they heard it, while the rest of us try to suppress our suicidal inclinations by thinking about the gin bottle at home. *(See also **Fike** and **Findy**, and also — if you really insist on following this one up — **Hoppestere**.)*

Absquatulate. (Ab-<u>skwo</u>-tyoo-laet) **vi**. *To make a hurried departure, with a usually unsuccessful attempt at doing so secretly*. The wholly predictable outcome, after years of misery for all concerned, of any American military invasion of another country.

Accoy. (A-<u>koy</u>) **vt**. *To render silent*.

> *Whilst it is hardly a matter of surprise that one should entertain wishful thoughts about accoying politicians, it is a little disconcerting that such ruminations should almost invariably be attended by images of guns, axes, and assorted forms of poison.*
>
> Herman von Halbricht
> *The Psychopathology of Politics* (2002)

Accurtation. (A-kur-<u>tae</u>-sh'n) **n**. *Shortening*. Can also mean 'reduction to nothing,' when applied to the process whereby the text of a speech made by a politician is abridged, leaving only those statements which refer to the actual practicalities of instituting a newly announced policy. *(See also **Agible** and **Yarely**.)*

Achroous. (<u>A</u>-kroe-us) **a**. *Colourless*. That aspect of life in Oldham that puts it one notch up on life in Accrington.

Acquest. (A-<u>kwest</u>) **n**. *Something that is acquired*. A term that is no longer useful in British schools when referring to the solution of simultaneous quadratic equations, the calculation of square roots, or even, God help us, to knowing that the difference between a colon and a semi-colon has nothing to do with resective surgery of the lower bowel.

Acrasy. (<u>A</u>-kra-see) **n**. *Disorder*. Also the name of the educational theory first put forward in 1962 by Edward J. Acras, which led to the replacement of rows of desks by randomly dispersed tables and chairs, and thus to the demise of the term 'acquest' *(q.v.)* in British schools.

Acturience. (Ak-<u>tyoor</u>-ree-'ns) **n**. *The desire to act*. A term used to describe the mental processes of the aspiring novelist, though seldom in close association with the words 'pen to paper.'

Adight. (A-<u>diyt</u>) **vt**. *To equip suitably*. A verb once used in relation to British military forces engaged in action overseas.

Adipsy. (<u>A</u>-dip-see) **n**. *A lack of thirst*. A concept unknown amongst journalists, professional footballers, and Celts of whatever calling.

Adminicle. (Ad-<u>mi</u>-ni-k'l) **n**. *That which provides support*. As, for example, a person who supports a colleague's bid for promotion, in the belief that such loyalty will subsequently be reciprocated. The term can also be used to mean 'a credulous person,' and 'one who is still wet behind the ears.'

Adrad. (A-<u>drad</u>) **a**. *Terrified*. May now be used to mean 'living in North Korea or Zimbabwe, or on the Old Kent Road.'

Aduncate. (<u>A</u>-dun-kaet) **a**. *Curving inward*.

> *The chicken that Ken Tuckie fried,*
> *And which with many chips he ate,*
> *Ensured that, though he quickly died,*
> *He was not ever aduncate.*

Adversion. (Ad-<u>ver</u>-sh'n) **n**. Attention.

> *We must all realise that a child's failure to pay attention to his*
> *parents, or to behave in a civilized fashion in the presence of*
> *other people, is a clear sign of adversion-deficit / hyperactivity*

disorder, and is therefore entirely understandable, no-one's fault, and always to be excused and tolerated with a benign smile.

Dr Sybil Flume
Modern Parenting (2005)

Affabrous. (<u>A</u>-f'-br's) **a**. *Workmanlike*. This term, which fell into disuse some thirty or more years ago in the UK, is once again coming into fashion, though it is now applied exclusively to persons with names ending in '-wicz.'

Affile. (A-f<u>iyl</u>) **vt**. *To sharpen*. Widely used until the late 1960s to describe what children did in school, as in the phrase 'to affile the wits,' the word is making a spirited comeback in inner-city schools, where pupils spend a substantial proportion of their day affiling blades of assorted lengths.

Afterclap. (<u>Af</u>-t'-klap) **n**. *That which occurs unexpectedly after an episode of activity has ended*. Also 'a sexually transmitted disease.'

Afterpiece. (<u>Af</u>-t'-pees) **n**. *In Edwardian times, a farce staged after the main performance of the evening*. A term that might well prove useful to psephologists to mean either (1) the counting of votes in Florida or any other third-world country; or (2) the casting of votes after a debate in the House of Commons.

Agamic. (A-g<u>a</u>-mik, *or* Ae-g<u>a</u>-mik) **a**. *Lacking the capacity for sexual activity.*

> He found that vintage cider,
> Through its actions hypothalamic,
> Augmented his libido,
> Though it rendered him agamic.

Agelast. (<u>A</u>-j'-last) **n**. *Someone who is not amused and does not laugh*. May be applied, for example, to a taxpayer who reads that the Arts Council has awarded a substantial grant to a 'talented performance artist' who intends to sit in the middle of Oxford Street with a toothbrush up each nostril.

Agerasia. (A-jer-<u>ae</u>-sha) **n**. *The quality of not ageing*. As may be used when wondering whether certain of those in the audience at an Oscars ceremony keep paintings in their attics that would frighten the living daylights out of you.

Aggrace. (A-<u>graes</u>) **vt**. *To favour one person over another*. An unpleasant aspect of behaviour in those in whom it occurs, this is never demonstrated by the cabin crew on low-cost flights, who are scrupulously even-handed in their dislike of everyone.

Agible. (<u>A</u>-ji-b'l) **a**. *Practicable*. A term ruled by the Speaker of the House of Commons in the late 19th century to be 'unparliamentary,' and which has therefore always subsequently been avoided when drafting an Act of

Parliament. It seems unlikely that this amiable little word will ever find employment in political circles. *(See also* **Accurtation** *and* **Yarely***.)*

Agnoiology. (Ag-noy-<u>o</u>-lo-jee) **n**. *The study of ignorance.*

> *Downing Street today denied that the change in the title of the Department for Education and Skills (DfES) to the Department of Children, Schools and Families (DCSF) was the first step in the elimination of the term 'education' in the UK. The denial followed reports that a government spokesman, in what was intended to be an off-the-record briefing, had commented that proposed changes to the core curriculum and the structure of examinations could well mean that the DCSF would have to be renamed the Department for Agnoiology.*
>
> National News Agency Report
>
> 15 January 2008

Aitch. (Aech) **n**. *The name of the letter 'H'.* This has now fallen into total disuse and has been replaced by the word 'haitch,' which means either 'The education I received didn't get as far as teaching me the alphabet,' or 'You can tell I'm educated, because I always pronounce my haitches.'

Aleuromancy. (A-<u>lyur</u>-oe-man-see) **n**. *The art of predicting the future by examining flour.* According to the political historian G. L. Ruggle, this is the only possible explanation for Britain's foreign policy throughout the 19th and 20th centuries. *(See also* **Alphitomancy***.)*

Alewife. (<u>Ael</u>-wiyf) **n**. *A woman in charge of an establishment selling ale*. A word that may be extended to mean 'anyone that it would be worth getting to know.' *(See also* **Brewster**.*)*

Algedonic. (Al-jee-<u>do</u>-nik) **a**. *Relating to both pleasure and pain*. Applicable especially to the description of a number of discreet establishments within a mile or so of the Palace of Westminster and which, although operating exclusively within the private sector, receive indirectly almost the entirety of their funding from the public purse.

Algist. (<u>Al</u>-jist) **n**. *A person who studies algae*. Or bankers.

Alloquial. (A-<u>loe</u>-kwee-al) **a**. *The manner in which one person addresses another*. According to the distinguished etymologist J. P. Prout, the word is a contraction of 'alloalloquial,' an interpretation adopted by a British television series documenting important aspects of social communication during the German occupation of France.

Alogotrophy. (A-loe-go-<u>go</u>-tro-fee) **n**. *Physical deformity induced by excessive nutrition*. A condition named after the American nutritionist Alan O. Gottrowe (1935–2002) who, in 1999, as an experiment, ate 43 beefburgers every day for ten months, eventually attaining the extraordinary weight of 948 pounds. When the block and tackle needed to move him collapsed under the strain, the huge pulleys bounced off his abdomen, leaving him unmarked and unharmed. *(See also*

Abdominous, Belue, Corsy, Fubsy, Lingism, Pinguescence
and *Saginate*.)

Alout. (A-<u>lowt</u>) **vi**. *To stoop*. A word known only in the UK,
where it used to be applied exclusively to the curious
crouching stance adopted by girls when playing the tradi-
tional game involving horse chestnuts, as in the phrase 'She
alouts to conkers.'

Alphitomancy. (Al-<u>fi</u>-toe-man-see) **n**. *Telling the future by
examining barley-meal*. G. L. Ruggle (1953), in his seminal
work, *Britain on the World Stage: 1849–1951*, claimed that
alphitomancy was adopted by the Foreign Office in 1945,
after it was finally concluded that the policy of basing international diplomacy on aleuromancy *(q.v.)* had proved disastrous. *(See also **Aleuromancy**.)*

Amenty. (A-<u>men</u>-tee) **n**. *Madness*. A chronic and intractable
delusional condition which, according to psychiatrists, is the
only possible explanation, not so much of the actual decisions
reached by Turner Prize judges, but of the judges' suitability
for undertaking the task in the first place. *(See also **Flitty**.)*

Amoinder. (A-<u>moyn</u>-der) **vt**. *To reduce or diminish*. A term
which, if reintroduced, would undoubtedly appear with great
regularity in local government documents relating to expenditure on socially important services, but which would never
be applied to discussions of the expense allowances of coun-
cillors or of the pensions arrangements of town hall staff.

Amphiboly. (Am-fi-bo-lee) **n**. *Ambiguity in a statement or utterance*. As Norma Hoole, in *English Humour* (2001), put it: 'It is a wonderful characteristic of the English language, and one that we must be careful to cherish and preserve, that, unlike those highly inflected tongues which allow for nothing but absolute precision of meaning, not only is amphiboly readily achieved, but, whether done so intentionally or inadvertently, it also provides enormous pleasure and entertainment.' Ms Hoole provided many examples, two of which are given here:

> *Mr Bullock was arrested by Constable Wright after he had driven his car through the plate-glass window of a butcher's shop.*
>
> Local news item broadcast on Tulip FM Radio
1 March 2000

> *Mr David Griffon, prosecuting, claimed that Mrs Freda Loynes (38) of 27 Bathfield Street had initiated a violent argument with her neighbour Mrs Burroughs, in the course of which she had torn open her blouse.*
>
> Report in the *Shropshire Bugle*
21 November 1992

Amphiscian. (Am-fish-'n) **n**. *An inhabitant of those equatorial regions where shadows sometimes fall to the north and at other times to the south*. Also 'a person with political ambitions.' *(See also* **Ascian**.*)*

Ampullosity. (Am-p'-<u>lo</u>-si-tee) **n**. *Inflated inanity*. Demonstrated in its most eloquent form when highly placed, but not medically educated, people talk about complementary medicine (and, in some cases, about anything else).

Anacoluthia. (A-na-ko-<u>loo</u>-thee-a) **n**. *A grammatical solecism in which a statement commencing with one construction ends with a different, and inappropriate, one*. Permission for research into the incidence of anacoluthia in GCSE English examination answers was withheld by the Chief Examiner because, in his words, 'There is not only little possibility of meaningful findings arising from this study and it is refused.'

Anchoret. (<u>An</u>-kor-ret) **n**. *A person who withdraws into seclusion from the world*. A most useful word which, in today's world, could have multiple alternative meanings, such as: 'a person of sensibility and discernment,' 'someone who jumps from a driverless train before it hits the buffers,' or 'the prime suspect.'

Anemious. (A-<u>nee</u>-mee-'s) **a**. *Windy, or preferring to exist in a place where there is a lot of wind*. A descriptive term applicable to those who believe in the usefulness of committees.

Anenterous. (An-<u>en</u>-ter-'s) **a**. *Having no guts*. A justifiable interpretation of the reason why a British government should insist upon complying to the last detail with every European Commission Directive, when, as everyone is perfectly well aware, these things are totally ignored by the French, and their very existence unknown to the Italians. *(See also **Aporrhœa** and **Fashious**.)*

Angary. (<u>An</u>-gar-ree) **n**. *The right assumed by belligerents to destroy the property of noncombatants*. A term that can usefully be applied more generally to any instance of having fun under the most unpromising of circumstances.

Anhistous. (An-<u>his</u>-t's) **a**. *Lacking any recognizable structure*. This term may be applied to a political party which, having discarded the policies that led to its being thrown out of office, is left bereft of ideas, and therefore attempts to recreate a structure for itself by thinking up new policies – even though to do so runs counter to the common belief that political parties are formed around ideals, and not the other way round.

Anientise. (A-nee-<u>en</u>-tiyz) **vt**. *To make something come to nothing*. As when an interesting and potentially valuable idea is evaluated by a committee.

Anile. (<u>A</u>-niyl) **a**. *Weak in the head*. An explanation – or an excuse – for visiting Wolverhampton twice.

Anoure. (A-<u>noor</u>) **vt**. *To worship*. To act in accordance with the sentiment that remains when supplication, self-interest, fear, and a desire to live for ever, have all been abstracted. *(See also **Hery**.)*

Apoious. (A-<u>poy</u>-*y*'s) **a**. *Inert; having no active qualities*. A term applicable to those members of the European Parliament who do not immediately demand the suspension of the un-elected European Commission until such time as the Commission's financial accounts for the past decade have been approved by the auditors.

Aporrhœa. (A-po-<u>ree</u>-a) **n**. *An unpleasant discharge*. An exceptionally useful descriptive term with a variety of potential uses in the modern world, including, for example: that for which a newspaper columnist is paid; any of the published sequels to *Gone With the Wind*; and a Directive of the European Commission. *(See also **Anenterous** and **Fashious**.)*

Aproctous. (A-<u>prok</u>-t's, *or* Ae-<u>prok</u>-t's) **a**. *Lacking an anus*. Although this condition is found only in certain invertebrate animals, research is currently ongoing into the possibility of inducing it in humans, with the aim of greatly reducing the length of debates in the House of Commons. *(See also **Astomatous**.)*

Argal (<u>Ar</u>-g'l) **n**. *A clumsy argument poorly founded in logic*. In general, any argument that has strong appeal to those of clumsy intellect. As, for example, that put forward in the report of the Warren Commission.

Argol. (<u>Ar</u>-gol) **n**. *Dried cow dung*. Curiously, in Uzbekistan this is the proprietory name of a breakfast cereal not unsimilar to what in the UK is called 'Weetabix.'

Ariolate. (<u>A</u>-ree-oe-laet) **vi/vt**. *To foretell on the basis of omens*. For example, the announcement of a new government 'initiative' on education may be taken as an omen predicting a further decline in the standards of literacy and numeracy amongst primary school children.

Artilize. (<u>Ar</u>-ti-liyz) **vt**. *To render something artificial*. An extended use of the name given to the naturally occurring process identified in 2001 by Dr Julius Artil, who showed that over the course of 24 hours nutrients migrate from ready-cooked meals to the packaging in which they are sold, leaving the food unchanged in outward appearance but containing only salt, sugar and preservative agents in a matrix of an unidentified substance to which Artil gave the name 'gleep.'

Artillerist. (Ar-<u>ti</u>-ler-ist) **n**. *One skilled in gunnery*. According to the etymologist J. P. Prout, in his book *A Word in Your Hearing* (1966), this is a compound noun dating back to the Roman occupation of the north-west of England. Prout notes that it is derived from 'artillus' and 'erista,' which are, respectively, the Latin words for 'liver' and 'pool.'

Ascensive. (A-<u>sen</u>-siv) **a**. *Showing a desire to move upwards.*

> FRANK WITHERSPOON BILSTHORPE. *The son of an out-of-work Biddulph miner, Frank Bilsthorpe's early life was marked by extreme poverty and deprivation. At the age of 17, however, he gained a scholarship to study at Oxford, where, after obtaining a first-class degree, he undertook postgraduate studies and was subsequently awarded his DPhil in Astrophysics. An enthusiastic mountaineer, he climbed every mountain in the Swiss and French Alps before he reached the age of 30. Following his marriage to Lady Sylvia, the only daughter of Lord and Lady Frassingham-Pudney, he became CEO of Frassingham Armaments Ltd, at that time a primary supplier of heavy military equipment to the Ministry of Defence. At the time of his death in 1983, during an unsuccessful attempt to set a new altitude record for a hot-air balloon, he was reportedly the sixth richest person in the UK.*
>
> An entry in Joanne Mindleford's
> *Ascensive Britons* (2005)

Ascian. (<u>A</u>-sh'n) **n**. *An inhabitant of the equatorial regions, who, because the sun is directly overhead, casts no shadow.* A person showing this quality in the UK should be approached with caution, and their reaction to garlic closely observed. *(See also* **Amphiscian**.*)*

Aselline. (<u>A</u>-se-liyn) **a**. *Pertaining to an ass.* A useful adjective to bear in mind when evaluating anything said by a person who speaks with the authority of social position.

Asitia. (A-<u>si</u>-sha) **n**. *A pathological loathing of food*. A condition manifested by a willingness to eat only substances that neither look nor taste as though they have any nutritional content, and which is regarded by social psychologists as explaining the popularity of takeaway meals.

Astatic. (A-<u>sta</u>-tik) **a**. *Unable or unwilling to remain in one place*. A term to be applied (preferably written on something heavy) to young children at a wedding.

Astomatous. (A-<u>stoe</u>-ma-t's) **a**. *Lacking a mouth*. A condition that is, unfortunately, no barrier to political discourse. *(See also **Aproctous**.)*

Astragalomancy. (A-<u>stra</u>-ga-loe-man-see) **n**. *The use of dice for the purposes of divination*. The basis of financial policy in governments of all political persuasions (or, if it's not, then clearly it would be worth giving it a try).

Ataraxy. (<u>A</u>-ta-rak-see) **n**. *The state of being free from any disturbance of mind*. A word that is now used only by medical practitioners when signing a death certificate.

Ateknia. (A-<u>tek</u>-nee-a) **n**. *Childlessness*. The term has also more general connotations, including 'desolation,' 'sadness,' 'loneliness,' but also 'happiness,' 'freedom,' and sometimes 'ecstasy.' The precise meaning appears to depend upon the age of the writer.

Atimy. (A̲-ti-mee) **n**. *A state of public disgrace, with the withdrawal of civil rights*. The fate that should have befallen successive ministers who have so spectacularly fouled up the UK farming industry, instead of promoting them to higher office (and, in one particularly notable case, to the rank of Foreign Secretary).

Atmolysis. (At-m̲o̲-li-sis) **n**. *The separation of unequally diffusible gases*. A term which the highly respected parliamentary commentator Matthew Henry Stannard, in his autobiography *Hot Air and Hogwash: A Wasted Life* (1999), suggested might also be applied to the process by which Hansard is produced.

Atwite. (A-tw̲iy̲t̲) **vt**. *To call another person a fool*.

> *'I am inclined,' the zealot said,*
> *'All people to atwite*
> *Who have their own ideas, and thus*
> *Can't see that I am right.'*
> *The people, hearing what he said,*
> *Did not think much of it.*
> *'And we're inclined,' they all replied,*
> *'To label you a twit.'*

Aucupate. (O̲r̲-kyoo-paet) **vi**. *To attempt to catch birds by lying in wait for them and using craft and guile*. It is reported that an increase in the consumption of alcohol by females in recent years has made the craft and guile unnecessary (and also that bit about lying in wait).

Auspicy. (<u>Or</u>-spi-see) **n**. *Divination based upon the behaviour of birds.* As, for example, predicting, on the basis of a female companion's consumption of Chardonnay, that a taxi driver will, at some time in the near future, say 'You're not putting your bird in here, mate. It's not worth the cost of cleaning it up,' and drive off.

Autexousy. (Or-<u>teks</u>-u-see) **n**. *Free will.* A term used with equanimity only by those who haven't thought things through. *(See also* **Ultroneous**.*)*

Auturgy. (<u>Or</u>-ter-jee) **n**. *The process of working with one's own hands.* May now be generalized to include other rarely seen forms of behaviour, such as cooking fresh vegetables, sitting at a table at mealtimes (or even owning a table), being courteous, and correctly using the gerund.

B

Babblative. (<u>Ba</u>-bla-tiv) **a**. *Showing a tendency to babble*. This is derived from the grammatical term 'ablative,' a confusing form of the noun, found in some inflected languages, that carries any or all of the connotations 'by,' 'with' or 'from,' either separately or simultaneously, and quite possibly both. The term is descriptive of the way in which junior cabinet ministers blather when shoved unwillingly into the front line to defend their superiors' unguarded and ill-thought-out comments. Babblative utterances are readily recognized: they usually commence with the phrase 'The Minister's comment has been taken out of context,' and go downhill from there on. *(See also **Coffle**.)*

Balatron. (<u>Ba</u>-la-tron) **n**. *A buffoon*. Balatron, having insulted Hera, Zeus's wife, was banished from Olympus and became a functionary in the local government of Athens, where he was responsible for changing the collection of household waste from weekly to fortnightly. The disastrous, and entirely predictable, consequences of this policy led to the name of Balatron becoming synonymous with 'buffoon.'

Baragouin. (Ba-ra-<u>gwin</u>) **n**. *Speech rendered unintelligible because of a person's accent, use of jargon, or both.* This word briefly entered the language in 1969, the year in which Professor A. J. Baragou, an astrophysicist born in Jamaica but, from the age of 15, brought up in Glasgow, had his invitation to deliver the BBC Reith Lectures withdrawn after the first one-hour lecture was broadcast worldwide without a single word being understood by anyone anywhere.

Barful. (<u>Bar</u>-ful) **a**. *Replete with hindrances.* Applicable to forms designed by two or more senior civil servants in the course of a convivial evening in the club lounge, and which elderly citizens of reduced circumstances are required to complete, without error or omission, in order to obtain financial assistance from the government.

Barmecide. (<u>Bar</u>-mi-siyd) **n**. *One who offers illusory benefits.* A word of Antipodean origin, this is derived from the name of Sidney Barmison, a 65-year-old Australian known locally as 'Barmy Sid.' Barmison made a fortune selling 'luxury after-life apartments (all local taxes included),' before retiring to a villa in Libya with his 18-year-old girlfriend, Gloria.

Barr. (Bar) **vi**. *To make the sound of an elephant.* A word for which there is not yet much call in the north of England, but which, if global warming lives up to its promise, may come in handy one day. *(See also* **Infaust**.*)*

Beaconage. (<u>Bee</u>-ko-nij) **n**. *A toll levied for the maintenance of beacons*. A term now useful for describing any singularly bizarre new tax thought up by a cash-hungry government.

Bedizen. (Bi-<u>diy</u>-z'n) **vi**. *To dress up in a particularly vulgar fashion*. A word that qualifies for inclusion in this book because, although it is still used when referring to actresses attending film premieres, they are aware neither of the word nor of the need for its existence.

Begunk (Bi-<u>gunk</u>) **vt**. *To delude someone.*

> *To live a life of luxury,*
> *The agèd Duke she wed,*
> *Inheriting a fortune when*
> *He finally dropped dead.*
>
> *'Ah, hussy!' cried the relatives,*
> *'The Duke you did begunk.*
> *Persuading that old gentleman*
> *You thought him quite a hunk.'*

Bein (Been) **a**. *Of pleasant demeanour*. Applicable generally to shop assistants in provincial France, but not a universally useful word in Britain.

Belomancy. (<u>Be</u>-loe-man-see) **n**. *Divining the future by means of arrows*. Adapted by the US military to involve the use of cruise missiles instead of arrows, belomancy is used by the

Pentagon to predict the consequences of foreign-policy decisions. Although the procedure has invariably been found hopelessly inaccurate, it has never been rejected.

Belue. (Be-<u>loo</u>) **n**. *A huge beast.*

> *Beware of the blubberous, bulging Belue.*
> *It's roughly the size of a bull caribou.*
> *Although it moves slowly, because it's so fat,*
> *It's perfectly able to squash you quite flat.*
> *It measures six feet (plus a bit) at the hips,*
> *Because it feeds only on burgers and chips.*
> *When passing fast-food shops, keep clear of the queue,*
> *For there lurks the blubberous, bulging Belue.*

Berattle. (Bi-<u>ra</u>-t'l) **vi**. *To rattle away.* A term that could be used to describe a diplomat's pointless involvement in a debate in the United Nations Security Council, when it is known by everyone that – as on all previous, and undoubtedly on all future, occasions – the outcome is predetermined by political considerations that have more to do with self-interest or testosterone (and most likely both) than with logic or justice. *(See also **Maffle**.)*

Beslaver. (Bi-<u>sla</u>-ver) **vi**. *To slaver over someone.* Those in a position to know about such things have described this as the most sophisticated of the amatory techniques that someone who has just downed half a dozen glasses of absinthe is capable of mustering.

Beslobber. (Bi-<u>slo</u>-ber) **vi/vt**. *To kiss like a drivelling child.*
This apparently comes a close second to beslavering.

Bever. (<u>Bee</u>-ver) **n**. *A small meal between main meals.* According
to research carried out by the Department of Nutrition at
the University of Rutland, in present-day Britain one person
in four takes just under three hundred bevers a day.

Birkie. (<u>Ber</u>-kee) **n**. *A confident man, with a mind of his own.*
If such a person were ever to be elected to the Papacy, he
would be able to do anything he wished, except buy life
insurance. *(See also **Vaticinate**.)*

Bismer. (<u>Biz</u>-mer) **n**. *A person deserving to be treated with scorn.*
A word that could be of considerable use to members of the
teaching profession, who would find it quicker to say than
'Secretary of State for Children, Schools and Families.'

Bittock. (<u>Bi</u>-tok) **n**. *A little bit.*

> *If you're lonely and you're feeling awful sad,*
> *If the rubbish on the telly drives you mad,*
> *And your life is in a pickle,*
> *Try a bit of slap and tickle,*
>
> *For a bittock of what you fancy does you good.*
> *When the day is dark and dreary, wet and cold,*
> *When the mirror says 'Oh God, you're getting old!'*

> *And you're nervous and you're jumpy,*
> *Try a bit of rumpy pumpy.*
> *Yes, a bittock of what you fancy does you good!*

(With apologies to the late Marie Lloyd.)

Blad. (Blad) **n**. *A hard blow or slap; also a lump of something.* Everyone can think of at least two people who would benefit greatly from a blad, preferably with a blad of something solid.

Blee. (Blee) **n**. *Complexion, particularly of the face.* Also a collective noun for cheap fat-based preparations of unpleasant odour, sold in small quantities in extraordinarily expensive glass bottles.

Boanthropy. (Boe-an-thro-pee) **n**. *A form of madness in which a person believes that he is an ox.* An illness that was thought to have died out, but which has shown a resurgence in Britain in recent years. The condition, which is of sudden onset, is particularly common amongst males frequenting city centres on Saturday nights.

Bolk. (Bolk) **vi**. *To vomit.* Applicable specifically to those suffering from boanthropy *(q.v.)*.

Bollen. (Bo-len) **a**. *Puffed up.* F. G. Grieber, in *The Origins of Parliamentary Language* (1992), suggests that 'politician' may have been derived from an earlier term, 'bollentician.'

Bonair. (Bon-<u>air</u>) **a**. *Courteous*. In the UK, refers to anyone who knocks you off the pavement just after a bus has passed. *(See also **Comity** and **Prosopolepsy**.)*

Bowssen. (<u>Bow</u>-s'n) **vt**. *To immerse someone in a well*. A once popular and highly enjoyable sporting activity, in which maximum points were awarded when the well was exceptionally deep and the person being dropped into it was about to embark upon a promising career in banking. There is currently much talk of reviving the sport, possibly to Olympic standard.

Brabble. (<u>Bra</u>-b'l) **vi**. *To engage obstinately in an argument concerning a trifling matter*. Specifically, to participate in a debate in the House of Lords.

Brewster. (<u>Broo</u>-ster) **n**. *A woman skilled in the art of brewing*. Often extended to include any female who dedicates her life to the preservation of the highest expressions of culture, and who, in the words of Schiller:

> *Sees, as in a crystal clear,*
> *Those things that menfolk hold most dear.*

*(See also **Alewife**.)*

Buckeen. (Bu-<u>keen</u>) **n**. *A young man who wishes to imitate the aristocracy*. Someone who has never taken a good long look at the aristocracy.

Bufflehead. (<u>Bu</u>-f'l-hed) **n**. *A stupid person*. Derived from the name of the educationalist M. K. T. Buffle, who, in 1962, was responsible for the replacement of the phonic technique by the 'look-and-say' method in the teaching of reading. Buffle argued that reading is primarily a matter of 'mentally feeling the shape of words,' and that it has little to do with individual letters and their associated sound values. The term is thus applicable: (1) to anyone who can't see the wood for the trees; and (2) to someone who hasn't yet figured out how to find their own backside.

Bulimy. (<u>Byoo</u>-li-mee) **n**. *A pathological hunger most commonly seen in mentally deranged persons.* The primary symptom of this condition being a willingness to eat porridge.

Bumbaze. (Bum-<u>baez</u>) **vt**. *To confuse or bamboozle someone.* Applicable specifically to the act of teaching a child to read without using phonics. *(See also **Bufflehead**.)*

Burd. (Berd) **n**. *A young woman.* A delightful word which allows one to deliver scathing (and, of course, carefully rehearsed,) ripostes to those of feminist inclination who object loudly to comments such as 'She's a really nice burd,' 'There's a new burd in the office,' and so on.

Buscarl. (<u>Bus</u>-karl) **n**. *A sailor*. One of the few words in the English language to have been taken from Finnish, this has not been used in the UK for over two hundred years. However, the softly spoken greeting 'Hello, Buscarl' may still be heard in the quaint, dimly lit streets leading from the Helsinki docks, as kindly Finnish gentlemen offer hospitality and friendship.

Buss. (Bus) **vt**. *To kiss with enthusiasm*. An act carried out by Italian men confronted with any living organism, and, for all I know, with dead ones.

C

Cab. (Kab) **vi/vt**. *To plagiarise*. Useful when referring to any document prepared with the help of the internet, but particularly to that which the British government presented in order to demonstrate conclusively that Saddam Hussein was planning to blow up the world.

Cachinnation. (Ka-ki-<u>nae</u>-sh'n) **n**. *Unnecessarily loud laughter*. As produced, for example, by MPs when the leader of their party makes a mildly amusing comment in the House of Commons. The word may still be heard occasionally on the hill farms of Cumbria, where it is used by farmers to refer to the sound made by sheep with digestive problems.

Cacotopia. (Ka-ko-<u>to</u>-pee-a, *or* Ka-koe-<u>toe</u>-pee-a) **n**. *A thoroughly evil place*. In *Unexplored Britain* (1950), the agoraphobic travel writer William Moal used the term 'cacotopia' to mean more or less anywhere outside a ten-yard radius of No. 32 Blueberry Avenue, Wigan.

Cadgy. (<u>Ka</u>-jee) **a**. *Amorously wanton*.

> EDWIN: In truth, I would take her to wife, were it not
> that she is so cadgy.
>
> WILLIAM: Amorously wanton?
>
> EDWIN: Aye.
>
> WILLIAM: There's many a man would welcome that!
>
> EDWIN: That, my friend, is what I fear!
>
> WILLIAM: Then change her.
>
> EDWIN: Change?
>
> WILLIAM: Aye. In your mind.
>
> EDWIN: How so?
>
> WILLIAM: See her not as amorously wanton, but as
> wantonly amorous.
>
> EDWIN: Genius, thy name is William!

Francis Theodore Payne

A Marriage of Inconvenience (1892)

Caducity. (Ka-<u>dyoo</u>-si-tee) **n**. *A tendency to fall over*.

RIP

GEORGE THRUMB

(1936–1989)

TO TRIM THE TREE HE THOUGHT TOO TALL,

HE STOOD ATOP THE GARDEN WALL,

BUT, CHOPPING, TO REDUCE IT, HE

FORGOT HIS OWN CADUCITY.

Cæspitose. (<u>Se</u>-spi-toes) **a**. *Growing in clumps.* A description of the hair that, for biologically obscure reasons, but probably something to do with evolutionary malevolence or the mark of Cain, appears in the ears and nose as men grow older.

Caggy. (<u>Ka</u>-gee) **a**. *Bad-natured.* A condition which a woman can inflict upon her unborn child by visiting Birkenhead.

Calamistrate. (Ka-la-<u>mi</u>-straet) **vi**. *To curl.* Describes what happens to one's toes when a politician tries to sound sincere.

Callet. (<u>Ka</u>-let) **n**. *A woman who behaves or speaks in an obscene manner.* One who has forgotten wherein lies the true strength of her sex. *(See also **Hoyden**.)*

Campaned (Kam-<u>paend</u>) **a**. *Furnished with bells.*

> *A butt he was of feeble jokes*
> *Of giggling girls and beery blokes.*
> *'Enough!' the maddened chap complained.*
> *'Just pull the other – it's campaned.'*

Capnomancy. (<u>Kap</u>-noe-man-see) **n**. *Divination by examining smoke.* For example, on observing thick black smoke pouring out of the Palace of Westminster, one might predict a bright and highly agreeable future for the country. *(See also **Ignicolist**.)*

Carny. (<u>Kar</u>-nee) **vi**. *To wheedle*. A low and demeaning form of behaviour, involving whining, grovelling and begging, in which politicians engage when trying to get elected – a revolting spectacle which the electorate ought to, but never does, remember. *(See also **Cuittle**.)*

Carotic. (Ka-<u>ro</u>-tik) **a**. *Possessing the power to stupefy or render unconscious.* Once limited mainly to powerful sedatives or blows to the head, this characteristic can now also be assigned to Council Tax bills. Not to be confused with 'erotic,' a quality observed in a Council Tax bill only by someone who is very, very sick.

Carriwitchet. (Ka-ree-<u>wi</u>-chet) **n**. *A pun.* A word first used by Tristram Foulds in *The Punning Plan*, a tiresome four-act play in which every sentence spoken contained at least one pun. In the final act, Gertrude, commenting upon the handbag being held by her aunt, Mrs Carriwitchet, goes on to ask 'And what do you carriwitchet?' The play, which was presented in 1921 at the Aldwych Theatre, London, had a run of only two performances, the second of which was cut short in the third act when the mood of the audience turned ugly.

Cartulary. (<u>Kar</u>-tyoo-la-ree) **n**. *A repository of papers and records.* Herbert Loomer, in *Where Words Come From* (1908), claimed that the origin of 'cartulary' lay in the mediæval Latin term for a horse-drawn cart in which rubbish was taken away to be burnt. However, Loomer was known to suffer from a florid allergic reaction to paper, and was accused by a contemporary etymologist, Florian Lambert, of having a jaundiced view of the matter.

Catachresis. (Ka-ta-<u>kree</u>-sis) **n**. *The abuse of words*. Catachresis – the ultimate horror in a society that has reduced education to a branch of the entertainment industry – may be either grammatical (as in 'I was sat,' 'we were stood,' 'a phenomena,' 'to commence a new build') or pronunciatory (as in '*dis*tribute,' '*con*tribute,' 'elec*to*ral,' 'ad*ve*rsary,' 'in*ve*ntory' and 'for*mi*dable'), but one would be prepared to overlook all of this, and more, for the correct use of the gerund – just once in a while.

Catasta. (Ka-<u>ta</u>-sta) **n**. *The dais on which slaves stood when being sold*. May now be applied to the stage on which aspiring young actors are auditioned.

Catharan. (<u>Ka</u>-tha-r'n) **n**. *A person who claims superiority over others in the matter of purity*. Useful for referring to particularly sanctimonious and moralizing priests – until they're caught in the vestry with three senior members of the Mothers' Union, or (which, when you think about it, is rather less disgusting) with the altar boy.

Certiorate. (<u>Ser</u>-shi-o-raet) **vi**. *To give information with great authority*. To bullshit.

Cervisial. (Ser-<u>vi</u>-sh'l) **a**. *Pertaining to beer.*

> He looks about with glazèd eye,
> His balance superficial,
> Too loose his tongue to frame a word —
> The shyndrome ish cervisial.

Chalastic. (Ka-<u>la</u>-stik) **a**. *Eliminating rigidity or stiffness.* Research conducted in the University of Chapeltown, Michigan, has recently shown that priapism may be substantially alleviated, and in some cases totally cured, by asking sufferers to call up a mental image of any lady novelist you care to name — thereby confounding W. S. Gilbert's view that, were such singular anomalies to cease to exist, they never would be missed.

Chavel. (<u>Cha</u>-v'l) **vi**. *To chatter.* A word widely used in the 16th century.

BEAUCHAMP: Dost ride, my Lord?
   E'en in the gloom of long-departed day?
CHESSINGHAM: Aye, and hastily, lest gloom
   Fall too upon our blighted land.
BEAUCHAMP: Then go with blessings,
   And return anon.
   'Tis noised that Aquitaine to Chateauville is gone
   Where Molinvar resides;
   And bids that dark and vengeful man
   Let slip the Frogs of war.
CHESSINGHAM: Then cease, good Sir, to chavel!
   To Paris shall I take my earnest plea.

> Those Frogs shall jump in very fear
> Ere dawning of another day they see!
>
> > Thomas Malvern
> > *William of France* (1578)

Chevise. (<u>Che</u>-viyz, *or* <u>She</u>-viyz) **vt**. *To bring something to a successful conclusion.*

> Dr Felton gave his considered professional opinion that the Prime Minister should be detained under the relevant sections of the Mental Health Act (1983, amended 2007), and that a detention order should be served without delay. Whilst he agreed that the Prime Minister had shown no further evidence of violent tendencies since the regrettable incident involving the Foreign Secretary, Dr Felton suggested that a persistence in asserting that the government's policies on health, education, the economy, foreign relations, and an integrated public transport system, either had been or ever could be chevised, could be taken as clear and incontrovertible evidence of a pathological detachment from reality. The members of the Tribunal, however, rejected this assessment and declined to issue an order for the detainment of the Prime Minister for a compulsory treatment period of six months.
>
> > Leaked Report of the Mental Health Tribunal
> > (Date deleted)

Chink. (Chink) **n**. *A fit of convulsive laughter accompanied by coughing and spluttering.* Specifically when reacting to the assertion that 'Made in China' is synonymous with quality.

Chopping. (<u>Cho</u>-ping) **a**. *Big and strapping*. A term that comes from the name of Wei Cho Ping, holder of the Chinese national record for the women's shot-put, who was arrested during the 1976 Olympic Games in Montreal after she had forcibly entered the offices of the *Quebec Star and Record* and broken the arms of four journalists and the legs of a further two. The newspaper had published a story the previous day expressing the view that Wei Cho Ping's claim to be a woman should be treated with caution.

Chouse. (Chows) **vt**. *To defraud*. To extract money from others by promising benefits which never materialize (and which, if one had thought carefully about it before handing over the cash, never had a hope in hell of ever doing so). The word can also be used to mean 'to levy taxes.'

Chrysostomic. (Kri-so-<u>stoe</u>-mik) **a**. *Exceptionally eloquent*. A word to be used primarily in the context of not turning your back on anyone to whom this may be applied. *(See also* **Facund**.*)*

Chuff. (Chuf) **n**. *A boorish or churlish person*. A most helpful word which not only denotes a person at whom a swift kick might usefully be directed, but also incorporates a hint as to where it might be aimed.

Cicurate. (<u>Si</u>-kyur-aet) **vt**. *To tame*. This word surfaced recently with the discovery of the earliest known draft of one of Shakespeare's plays, which was found amongst other documents of historical interest in the attic of Helmsbridge House in Bedfordshire, where the Bard was known to have occasionally stayed. The draft, written in the playwright's own hand, carried the title *Cicuration of the Vole*, which had been crossed out and replaced by *Taming of the Dormouse*.

Circue. (<u>Ser</u>-kyoo) **vi**. *To go round.*

THE FABLE

> *The Education Minister*
> *Thought long and hard and deep.*
> *'How can we make our schools succeed*
> *And learning standards leap?'*
> *He put the question ceaselessly*
> *To everyone he met,*
> *But not a single sensible*
> *Response could ever get.*
> *Until one day he met a man*
> *Who told him what to do.*
> *'Put desks in rows, and buy some pens,*
> *Some chalk, and blackboards too.*
> *Buy lots of paper – ruled, not plain –*
> *And teach the kids to read*
> *From proper books and not from screens.*
> *Success is guaranteed.'*
> *The Minister just laughed, and said,*
> *'That's not the modern way.'*
> *The man replied, 'Do not reject*

Techniques of yesterday
That many scholars once inspired
And Nobel prizes brought.
Such pupils weren't just entertained,
Or by computers taught!'
The Minister said, 'Very well,
Your methods we shall use.
We might as well give them a shot —
We've bugger all to lose.'
Within a year or two, at most,
The tide completely turned:
No child there was who could not read;
No maths remained unlearned.

THE MORAL

What circued once can circue twice.
And (this one can't deny)
In education, as in life,
It's always worth a try.

Civism. (Si̱-vi-z'm) **n**. *The ideals of good citizenship*. The introduction of 'citizenship' as a core curriculum subject in British schools has had the gratifying result of persuading twelve-year-old artillerists *(q.v.)* in Liverpool to say 'sorry' after shooting people.

Clamjamphrie. (Klam-ja̱m-free) **n**. *Twaddle*. This is a useful word, as, for example, in such phrases as 'The chairman thanked the vicar for his illustrated clamjamphrie,' 'There now follows a Party Political Clamjamphrie,' and 'The Man Booker Prize for Fiction was won by Gertrude Frumm, the judges unanimously praising her new international best-selling clamjamphrie.'

Clancular. (<u>Klan</u>-kyoo-lar) **a**. *Secret*. A word that could well be revived in the form of the title 'Her Majesty's Clancular Service,' coming, as it does, from the same root as 'clanger' (as dropped spectacularly by the Clancular Service when providing intelligence about atom bombs buried in sand).

Claver. (<u>Klae</u>-ver) **n**. *An item of gossip*.

> *'What headline shall we run today?*
> *The bombing in Iraq?*
> *The rescue from that burning ship?*
> *The moon (it's turning black)?*
> *The deadly flu that's going round?*
> *The flood that's drowned a village?*
> *The lorry that destroyed a bridge?*
> *That case of toxic spillage?'*
> *The Editor said, 'None of those.'*
> *He didn't even waver.*
> *'Forget all that. Our readers want*
> *A bit of juicy claver.'*

Clod-pate. (<u>Klod</u>-paet) **n**. *A thickhead*. In the UK, applicable especially to anyone who has been involved in improving the school curriculum over the last couple of decades.

Clour. (Kloor) **vt**. *To cause a lump to be raised on someone's head.* Also, to take appropriate action on encountering a clod-pate *(q.v.)*

Clumse. (Klums) **a**. *Idle.* A most useful word for those who value economy of expression: thus, in the statement 'I work no more than thirty hours a week, because I am asserting my fundamental human right to leisure time,' the last eight words can be replaced by 'clumse.'

Clunch. (Klunch) **n**. *A lout.* Specifically, a person who cannot understand why anyone would wish to buy and keep a book, now that it is possible to store its content in electronic form and read it on a computer screen.

Cockalorum. (Ko-ka-<u>lor</u>-rum) **n**. *A little man full of his own importance.*

HITLER [*thoughtful*]: Zis vurd everyvon use …
GOEBBELS: Vot vurd, mein Führer?
HITLER: Zat vurd – 'Führer.'
GOEBBELS [*puzzled*]: Ja?
HITLER: I don't like it.
GOEBBELS: You don't?
HITLER: Nein.
GOEBBELS: Vy not?
HITLER: It sounds like somevon clear der throat. [*Makes a hacking sound*]
GOEBBELS: Zo?

HITLER: I vont another vurd.

GOEBBELS: Vot vurd?

HITLER [*stamping his foot*]: How do I know? Idiot. Tink of von! Look at me – vot you see, huh?

GOEBBELS [*under his breath*]: A cockalorum!

HITLER [*hearing him*]: Ja! Das ist gut! I like it. [*Stamps about the room, crowing*] Cockalorum! Cockalorum!

GOEBBELS: Heil Cockalorum!

HITLER: Danke.

GOEBBELS [*relieved to have got away with it*]: Bitte!

Alan Freebles

Hitler at Home (1977)

Coffle. (<u>Ko</u>-f'l) **n**. *A group of beasts or slaves caused to move in the same direction.* In a government memo leaked to the press on 22 May 2007, the term 'electorate' had been crossed out, apparently by the Home Secretary, and 'coffle' inserted. A junior minister, interviewed on the *Today Programme* the following morning, insisted that the matter had 'been taken out of context.' *(See also* **Babblative**.*)*

Cogger. (<u>Ko</u>-ger) **n**. *Someone who flatters falsely.* The origins of the word are obscure, though perhaps the best explanation was given by Sir Graham Frobisher, one-time Minister for Transport, who reported that, at a meeting of the Cabinet in the late 1960s, the Home Secretary said to the Prime Minister, 'We humble members of the Cabinet are but cogs in a great administrative machine, of which you, sir, are the engine.' Also sometimes used as the verb 'to cogger,' meaning 'to cause anyone within earshot to throw up.'

Cogitabund. (<u>Ko</u>-jee-ta-bund) **a**. *Deep in thought*. Unlikely to be particularly useful when referring to anyone responsible for changes in social policy. *(See also **Yarely**.)*

Coll. (Kol) **vt**. *To embrace or hug someone*. According to the July 2008 issue of the trade journal *Cosmetics Weekly*, an 'anti-coll' spray has been developed and will be marketed within the next year or so under the name of 'Italianoff.' *(See also **Buss**)*.

Comeling. (<u>Kum</u>-ling) **n**. *An immigrant*. The word can now be extended to mean a shop assistant who is well-spoken, cheerful and helpful, and doesn't turn her back on you the moment she's slammed your money in the till. *(See also **Bein**.)*

Comity. (<u>Ko</u>-mi-tee) **n**. *Courtesy*. On the principle, first enunciated by Walter J. Alphonsus (*An Analysis of Conceptual Understanding*, 1908), that an abstract concept is best defined by the difference between its antithesis and its absence, it is instructive to distinguish between 'discourtesy' and 'a lack of courtesy.' To describe an act as being one of discourtesy presupposes some degree of thought behind the act's commission. However, having regard to the lack of evidence that, in the modern world, any actions are actually preceded by thought, one is driven to the conclusion that those thirteen-year-old schoolgirls who walk four abreast on the pavements of Lancaster, forcing everyone else to walk in the gutter or in the path of oncoming four-by-fours, do so not because they are intentionally discourteous, but because they haven't the merest inkling of what courtesy actually is – and no-one, it seems, has any interest whatsoever in imparting this information to them, or regards it as an important part of what is supposed to be their education. *(See also **Bonair** and **Prosopolepsy**.)*

Compesce. (Kom-<u>pes</u>) **vt**. *To curb or restrain*. A tendency which, in the mothers of three-year-olds, is rendered inoperative in supermarkets, apparently by something in the air.

Compt. (Kompt) **a**. *Dressed trimly, sprucely*. A word which may be applied to almost all who live and work in Paris, but which is of virtually no use at all in Blackpool. *(See also **Gim**.)*

Concinnate. (Kon-<u>si</u>-naet) **vt**. *To fit something together exactly*.

Dr Burroughs, a consultant psychiatrist, appearing as an expert witness on behalf of the defence, said he had no doubt that it had been Mr Grufton's repeated attempts, over a three-day period, to concinnate the MFI wardrobe that had caused him to act in the manner leading to his arrest. Dr Burroughs added that Mr Grufton had suffered additional trauma as a result of his having had to be restrained by the police and forcibly sedated.

Report in the *Eccles Star and Herald*
15 September 2002

Conculcate. (Kon-<u>kul</u>-kaet) **vt**. *To tread underfoot*. A useful alternative to the verb 'to govern.'

Conditory. (<u>Kon</u>-dit-or-ee) **n**. *A repository for the dead*. Derived from 'Condicester,' the name given by the Roman Emperor Claudius to what is now Bournemouth.

Conjobble. (Kon-<u>jo</u>-b'l) **vi/vt**. *To discuss*. May be used to describe what MPs do in a parliamentary debate. Can also mean 'to make a great show of considering an issue about which, as everyone is perfectly well·aware, a decision has already been made.' *(See also* **Berattle** *and* **Maffle**.*)*

Contabescent. (Kon-ta-<u>be</u>-s'nt) **a**. *Having wasted away or atrophied*. As applied, for example, to the average British person's knowledge of, concern about, or, indeed, the slightest interest in, English grammar.

Contection. (Kon-<u>tek</u>-sh'n) **n**. *The act of covering up*. In the UK, that process of government without which the members of the electorate would know for certain what they have always suspected.

Corsy. (<u>Kor</u>-see) **a**. *Fat*. Information obtained under the terms of the Freedom of Information Act reveals that if Wales, Scotland and Northern Ireland all attain independence, the government will propose that England be renamed. Of the various proposed alternative names, Lagerland, Loutland, and Euro-Unit Number Twelve have all been rejected in favour of Corsyland.

Coryphæus. (Ko-ri-<u>fee</u>-us) **n**. *The leader of a political party*. A Greek term, the most recently recorded use of which was in the UK General Election of 11 June 1987, when the New Hellenic Party put up eight candidates. The party's policy of restoring parliamentary democracy along the lines of the ancient Greek republic failed to capture the imagination of the electorate, and all eight candidates lost their deposits. The Coryphæus, Markos Dimitriopoulos, shot himself.

Creticism. (<u>Kre</u>-ti-si-z'm) **n**. *Lying*. Behaviour which, on the Hawsley-Newton Scale of Moral Rectitude, is two steps up from literary criticism.

Crool. (Krool) **vi**. *To make a prolonged, rather liquid, inarticulate sound*. As, for example, that made by farmers when asked to comment upon the latest government policy relating to the agricultural industry. *(See also **Estrepement** and **Pabulous**.)*

Cruentous. (Kroo-<u>en</u>-t's) **a**. *Bloody*. An adjective usually placed before 'politicians,' 'cyclists' and 'psychologists.'

Cuittle. (<u>Kyoo</u>-t'l) **vi**. *To wheedle*. The common cuttlefish, *Sepia officinalis*, entices small fish (its primary food) out of crevices in coral reefs by releasing scraps of food from its mouth. The verb 'to cuttle,' meaning 'to wheedle by the false promise of favours,' was first used by the Scottish naturalist Walter K. McBride, who devoted his life to the study of *Sepia*. The transformation of the spelling to 'cuittle' reflects its pronunciation amongst McBride's compatriots, to whom its use was mainly confined. *(See also **Carny**.)*

Culbut. (<u>Kul</u>-b't) **vt**. *To put to disorderly flight*. A verb for which, curiously, the French and Italian equivalents exist only in the first person, passive voice.

Cully. (<u>Kul</u>-ee) **n**. *A simpleton*. This comes from Mrs Flora May Enderby's romantic novel *Time and Tide* (1863) in which the central character was Thomas Cully, an octogenarian gardener who believed everything that he was told, however absurd or illogical it might be. The only other recorded instance of its use was in 1931 when it appeared in the first edition of Marcus Fothergale's influential textbook *The British Constitution*; however, in the second edition, published two years later, it was removed and replaced by the word 'voter.'

Cultch. (Kulch) **n**. *Rubbish*. Introduced into English during the time of the Raj, this word was taken from one of the minor languages of the Indian subcontinent, where its original meaning was 'fried chicken.' *(See also **Mullock** and **Peltry**.)*

Cumble. (<u>Kum</u>-b'l) **vt**. *To topple from power*. Curiously, this verb is often used when referring to US policy towards tyrants in Middle Eastern states, but never in relation to those who are to be found, in considerably greater numbers, in Africa.

Custron. (<u>Kus</u>-tron) **n**. *A cad*.

> Sir Alfred was a bounder,
> A swindler and a custron,
> His luxury apartment
> A temple to seduction.
>
> For there he lured young ladies
> With promises of riches.
> He said, when called a scoundrel,
> 'I scratch it where it itches.'
>
> He lived his life for pleasure,
> Was always hale and hearty,
> And like most other custrons,
> He joined the Tory Party.
>
> His character was spotted,
> And soon he was selected;
> Then, at a by-election,
> To parliament elected.
>
> His rise within the party
> He fixed by fixing others –
> A model modern Tory
> (They'd sacrifice their mothers).

But he who gains the summit
Must be prepared to handle
Whatever's least expected –
Particularly scandal.

Those ladies he had promised
A life of milk and honey
Sold out to Sunday tabloids
For record sums of money.

Their stories hit the headlines;
No details were omitted
Of women, wild and willing,
Debaucheries committed.

Next day, the Queen accepted
Sir Alfred's resignation;
'The House of Lords,' she told him,
'Is now your destination.'

For that's the way it happens
(Though hardly democratic) –
When social class is threatened,
Survival's axiomatic.

Lord Alfred's doing nicely
(No custron heeds life's hitches),
And still lures pretty ladies
With promises of riches.

D

Daddle. (<u>Da</u>-d'l) **vi**. *To walk unsteadily*. A commonly used word of north Lancashire origin, useful in referring to the mode of progression of half of those on the streets of Morecambe after ten o'clock at night.

Dade. (Daed) **vt**. *To support someone who is walking unsteadily*. This can be used when speaking of the other half. *(See **Daddle**.)*

Daggle. (<u>Da</u>-g'l) **vt**. *To drag through the mire*. May most usefully be used in the compound word 'daggle-glee,' which refers to the pleasure taken by British tabloid newspapers in daggling their latest victim. There is, however, no verb in the English language which adequately describes the delight of the tabloids' readers in seeing someone comprehensively daggled.

Dandizette. (Dan-dee-<u>zet</u>) **n**. *A female dandy*. In Yorkshire, this can be applied to a female in an Oxfam shop who selects clothes on the basis of fit.

Dauby. (<u>Dor</u>-bee) **a**. *Inclined to daub*. A useful descriptive term applicable to those who produce paintings with titles such as 'Blue Square' and 'Exegesis No. 6.' Oh, and while we're on the subject, anyone who calls a painting 'Untitled' should be led away and put down.

Deasil. (<u>Dee</u>-z'l) **a**. *Inclining towards the right*. As distinct from Evil (inclining towards the wrong).

Debell. (Dee-<u>bel</u>) **vt**. *To vanquish by force of arms*. A concept taught from a theoretical perspective in American military academies.

Decharmed. (Dee-<u>charmd</u>) **a**. *Disenchanted*. Useful in describing the state of the people about six months after they have ousted a repressive and corrupt regime and handing power over to those promising social and political reform.

Decrassify. (Dee-<u>kra</u>-si-fiy) **vt**. *To remove anything gross or offensive*. That which the electorate attempts to do at every general election, but, whatever the outcome, always without success. *(See also **Decharmed**.)*

Dedition. (Di-<u>di</u>-sh'n) **n**. *Surrender*. The only military stratagem available to those who march honestly, and with understanding, under the banner of Christianity.

Dedolent. (<u>De</u>-do-l'nt) **a**. *Callous*. Applicable to anything made hard by friction, or, in the case of a literary critic, by fiction.

Defedation. (Dee-fe-<u>dae</u>-sh'n) **n**. *Pollution*.

A RANT

It's amazing that a nation
Wading deep in defedation
And in piles of fast-food wrappers
Thrown from cars by fat old slappers,
Hasn't figured a solution
To the problem of pollution,
When there's CC television
That could spot, with fair precision,
Any yob who's dumping litter,
Then convey to a transmitter,
An instruction electronic
To destroy the slob moronic –
With a simple little bullet
Through their simple little skull. It
Wouldn't be expensive,
And not nearly as offensive
As the cans and plastic bags
And the empty packs of fags
And the bottles, and the boxes
Torn apart by rats and foxes
And ... et cetera.

Defossion. (Di-<u>fo</u>-sh'n) **n**. *The state of being buried alive.* Also the feeling of suffocation induced in members of the teaching profession by documentation sent to them from the Department of Children, Schools and Families (formerly the Department of Education – *see* **Agnoiology**) telling them (1) what to teach; (2) how to teach it; (3) what educationally irrelevant information to collect, document and submit (though no-one will have the time to read it); (4) to use computers under any circumstances where paper and pencil might suffice; and (5) to engage, motivate, excite and entertain their pupils whilst simultaneously fending off attacks by those armed with knives and a variety of blunt instruments.

Deipnosophist. (Diyp-<u>no</u>-s'-fist) **n**. *An expert in the art of dining.* A term still used in Huddersfield to describe a person who holds the view that one should add either ketchup or mustard, but not both, to a hotdog, in order to appreciate the full subtlety of flavour of that dish.

Dejerate. (<u>De</u>-jer-raet) **vi**. *To swear solemnly.* As, for example: 'I do hope that you will take my request in the altogether serious and nonconfrontational spirit in which it is meant, when I ask you to bugger off.'

Deleniate. (Dee-<u>le</u>-nee-aet) **vt**. *To soothe someone's feelings.* That which was at one time achieved by an apology, an expression of regret or remorse, or even a small act of kindness and generosity, but which can nowadays be accomplished only through a process of litigation followed by the award of substantial financial compensation.

Deme. (Deem) **n**. *A referee*. A person who is a completely impartial and totally unbiased judge of the conduct of an individual or group of individuals. The term may also be used to mean 'one who is not of this Earth.'

Deperition. (Dee-per-<u>ri</u>-sh'n) **n**. *A state of total wasting away*. That which one immediately knows has happened to standards in any public-service (as, for example, schools, universities, medical care, the police force, public libraries, the postal system, public-service broadcasting, and so on) as soon as any government minister starts to talk about how much money has been poured into it since his party came to power.

Dern. (Dern) **n**. *A secret*. Applies particularly to an item of information of a personal, confidential, sensitive and intimate nature which is never divulged to anyone (except, under threat of imprisonment, to any government department that asks for it so that it can then be sent by e-mail or post to all other government departments, none of which requested, needs, or has the faintest idea what to do with it). Also means 'a topic of conversation in every bar in Naples.'

Derve. (Derv) **vi**. *To labour*. As in the phrase 'to derve under the misapprehension that, once in the hands of a government department, anything can ever remain a dern *(q.v.).' (See also* **Salvatory***.)*

Desight. (Dee-<u>siyt</u>) **n**. *An eyesore*. A term that can usually be applied to any building that is described by architects as being 'iconic.'

Devel. (<u>De</u>-vel) **n**. *A forceful or stunning blow*. That which ought to be applied to anyone who would ever use a word like 'iconic.'

Dictery. (<u>Dik</u>-ter-ree) **n**. *A witty comment*. Oscar Wilde, an acknowledged master of the dictery, was given to making them so frequently that Lord Mallard (who detested Wilde) once referred to him as the 'head dicterist,' and, in a letter to the socialite Mrs Muriel Weatherspoon (whose intellectual accomplishments did not embrace wordplay of any but the most direct kind), as 'that old dictery head.'

Dight. (Diyt) **vt**. *To prepare, or make ready*.

> *He waiteth in the carriage stille,*
> *Yet of his wyfe there be no sight.*
> *'Oh why,' he cryeth, 'doth she take*
> *So many hours herselfe to dight?'*

Lord Slingsby

Collected Poems (1669)

Dindle. (<u>Din</u>-d'l) **vi/vt**. *To vibrate as a result of a percussive sound.*

> *Mr Scroot told the court that the radio of the parked car was so loud that the vehicle's roof was throbbing. He had therefore opened the door on the driver's side and said to the six youths inside, 'I think your car is dindling.' The youths, who cannot be named for legal reasons, are all charged with occasioning actual bodily harm.*
>
> Report in the Cumbria Star
> (8 July 2007)

Dirdum. (<u>Der</u>-d'm) **n**. *An outcry.* What should have occurred, but inexplicably didn't, following the issue of the Hutton Report on the death of Dr Kelly, which failed to explain (or, indeed, even to ask) why, if that unfortunate man had died, as stated by the pathologist who conducted the post-mortem examination, as a result of loss of blood, there was little or no blood reported where the body was found.

Divagate. (<u>Diy</u>-va-gaet) **vi**. *To wander.* As in the line 'I divagated lonely as a vaporous nebulosity' from the poem by Albert Wordsworth, William's second cousin once (and quite rightly) removed.

Dizzard. (<u>Di</u>-zard) **n**. *A dolt.* Used to refer to someone rather further gone than a bufflehead *(q.v.)*, and therefore destined for high political office.

Docible. (<u>Do</u>-si-b'l, *or sometimes, and perhaps preferably*, <u>Doe</u>-si-b'l) **a**. *Capable of being taught*. It was the assumption that this quality is shared by all pupils that led to the decision in the UK to encourage 50% of them to go on to university. As a consequence, although 'docible' was at one time applicable to all but a minority of university students, it is now a term of little use in academe. *(See also **Idoneousness** and **Indocibility**.)*

Doddypoll. (<u>Do</u>-dee-pol) **n**. *A blockhead*. Substantially worse than being a dizzard *(q.v.)*. A term that will, or so I'm informed, soon be used in the betting profession for anyone whose chances of becoming prime minister are so great that all bets on the matter will be refused.

Dolose. (Do-<u>loez</u>) **a**. *Deceitful*. The psychologist Chaim Reisenberg, on the basis of a study involving several hundred industrialists and entrepreneurs, concluded that deceitfulness was the most powerful predictor of success in commerce. A score of 95% or higher on the Reisenberg Dolosity Scale is required for entry into the London College of Advertising.

Downlooked. (<u>Down</u>-lookt) **a**. *Demure*. Applicable to any female aged between 16 and 30 who would be reluctant to reveal more than 90% of her body surface area in public. A word that finds little use in Carlisle.

Draffsack. (<u>Draf</u>-sak) **n**. *A paunchy glutton.*

> *Ms Petunia Fosworth-Gore, who was recently appointed Director for Sex Equality (England), has drawn attention to the nondiscriminatory value of the term 'draffsack.' Male and female draffsacks, she noted in her latest report, are physically more or less indistinguishable from each other, except on intimate medical inspection (and sometimes even then with difficulty). Bearing this in mind, and taking into consideration the virtual ubiquity of what used to be called 'obesity' but which, in line with European Directive 7667/33, is now to be called 'up-somatizing,' the utility of 'draffsack' has been formally recognized by Her Majesty's Government. As from 3 April 2010, city council officials throughout England will be required to use the term in preference to 'Sir,' 'Madam,' 'Mr,' 'Mrs,' 'Miss,' or 'Ms.' All official letters sent to members of the public will thus commence 'Dear Draffsack.'*
>
> Home Office Memorandum 7762F/3/08
> 14 June 2008

Dree. (Dree) **vi**. *To hold out, though suffering miserably*. This would certainly be useful in any sentence in which the words 'musical extravaganza' and 'village hall' were to appear together.

Dretch. (Drech) **vt**. *To afflict*. That which xylophone players are permitted to do with impunity to innocent people, but which ought, in all honesty, to lead to a charge of assault with a deadly weapon. *(See also **Xylophone**.)*

Droil. (Droyl) **vi**. *To drudge*.

> *Or, if the droiling be done without causing harm to others, to be a lexicographer.*
>
> James Boswell
> *The Life of Samuel Johnson, LL.D.* (1791)

Dub. (Dub) **vi**. *To pay up*. What, according to my calculation, I shall have to do, by means of my television licence fee, for the rest of my life, and for thirty-three thousand years after that (if you think I'm exaggerating, do the sum for yourself), in order to pay the salary of one well-known television personality for one year. It is not entirely coincidental that, in some thirty million homes, 'to dub' has come to mean 'to strike like a viper at the off-button on the TV remote control.'

Dulcarnon. (Dul-<u>kar</u>-non) **n**. *A dilemma*. A dulcarnon which faces many millions of people in the UK at the present time is whether to continue to dub *(q.v.)* for the excessive salaries of television 'celebrities' or shoot themselves now.

Dunch. (Dunch) **vt**. *To jab sharply with the elbow*. A reflex movement elicited in French people by the arrival of any form of public transport.

Dwale. (Dwael) **n**. *Sleep of the dead*. The medical term for the condition induced within five minutes by taking a dose of a strong barbiturate. The National Institute for Health and

Clinical Excellence (NICE) has, however, recommended that, for reasons of cost-effectiveness, prescriptions for barbiturates should be replaced by vouchers for the CD entitled *Interviews with Football Team Managers*, research having shown that dwale is induced within five seconds of putting on the CD (and sometimes simply by reading the label).

Dwine. (Dwiyn) **vi**. *To pine away*.

> *For love of her he could not have,*
> *He lay abed to dwine.*
> *He could not work, nor could he rest,*
> *But fell to gin and wine.*

Dysteleology. (Dis-tee-lee-o-lo-jee) **n**. *The view that nature is essentially purposeless*. After considering the existence of functionless rudimentary organs, or (which amounts to much the same thing) listening to a few minutes of a speech by any politician, one can see the appeal of such a doctrine.

E

Eadi. (<u>Ee</u>-dee) **a**. *Wealthy*. Describes a condition once believed to result from work, but now universally regarded as attainable only by correctly predicting a series of numerals, or (which there is a greater chance of doing) by becoming a professional footballer.

Educated. (<u>Edd</u>-yoo-kae-t'd) **a**. *Having been taught or trained*. An obsolete word to be removed from all English dictionaries. (Edyookaetd, incidentally, has become the preferred spelling in schools, amongst the 10 per cent of pupils who can write.)

Edulcorate. (Ee-<u>dul</u>-kor-raet) **vt**. *To ensure the removal of hard bits*. A process which, in the UK, has been applied, at the behest of politicians, to the school curriculum, in the hope that pupils, finding lessons easier and thus more 'entertaining,' might be less inclined to stab their teachers. As could have been predicted, insulting children by treating them as being intellectually on a level with politicians has had a result entirely opposite to that intended; despite this, the process of edulcoration is being intensified rather than abandoned.

Effate. (E-<u>fae</u>t) **n**. *A maxim*. A statement which succinctly expresses a moral or ethical precept: as, for example, 'If there is a single child living in poverty in this country, that child's circumstances must take priority over all else when it comes to determining public expenditure.' No doubt a notice saying this sits on the desk of the Prime Minister and on those of all members of his Cabinet, together with a little yellow Post-it sticker carrying a reminder that the word 'all' includes government IT projects, ministerial trips to far-off places, opulent refurbishment of grace-and-favour apartments and foreign 'aid' paid to corrupt regimes.

Efferous. (<u>E</u>-fer-r's) **a**. *Fiercely violent*. One wonders what might be meant by 'gently violent' or 'mildly violent.' The distinction between 'violent' and 'fiercely violent' may be of consuming interest to linguistic philosophers, but is, one suspects, of considerably less importance to a person encountering either in a dark alley.

Eident. (<u>Iy</u>-d'nt) **a**. *Attentive*. A term of little value in primary schools in the UK, since to be attentive implies to be still and quiet and to listen to what someone else is saying – all of which contravene what some demented European Commissioner has decided is a child's fundamental human right to be hyperactive.

Eirenicon. (Iy-<u>ree</u>-ni-kon) **n**. *A proposal to reconcile differences.* In diplomacy, that which is usually held back until bloodshed has been given an opportunity to do the trick.

Elench. (Ee-<u>lenk</u>) **n**. *A logical refutation of an argument.* Also a medical condition causing deafness in politicians.

Elenge. (<u>Ee</u>-lenj) **a**. *Over-long, tedious and dreary.*

> *Miss Wormsley compresses into just over four hundred pages what a lesser author would have required at least fifty pages to convey. In the hands of this author, whose command of vocabulary is such that there must surely be little room left in her mind for aught else, every word carries a deep and, at least to this reviewer, a hitherto unrecognized significance. Indeed, in this novel of unrequited love amongst the Laplanders, even the indefinite article is strangely elenge.*
>
> Henrik Van Rijn
> Book review in the *Edinburgh Literary Record*
> (3 October 1904)

Elinguate. (Ee-<u>lin</u>-gyoo-aet) **vt**. *To remove the tongue.*

> *Professor Edwin McMurphy FRCS, in a report submitted to the Royal College of Surgeons, has drawn attention to the inexplicably large number of politicians who have been accidentally elinguated whilst undergoing surgical procedures anatomically unconnected with the face.*
>
> *Weekly Medical News*
> (23 March 2006)

Elucubration. (Ee-loo-kyoo-<u>brae</u>-sh'n) **n**. *A literary work resulting from great mental effort*. Not necessarily, though, a great literary work.

Elumbated. (<u>Ee</u>-lum-bae-t'd) **a**. *Rendered weak in the loins*. An effect produced in men by women who, as a consequence of cosmetic surgery, have been rendered stiff in the face.

Emarcid. (Ee-<u>mar</u>-sid) **a**. *Wilted*. That condition which, when it occurs in plants, may usually be cured by the provision of an appropriate liquid. The similarities between plants and humans are often striking.

Emunge. (Ee-<u>munj</u>) **vi/vt**. *To cheat*. As, for example, to charge tuition fees for a three-year university degree in a subject that could be mastered in a couple of weeks by someone capable of holding a book the right way up, though not necessarily also of reading the big words in it.

Enchiridion. (En-kiy-<u>ri</u>-di-'n) **n**. *A technical manual or handbook*. A document in which the first instruction, when followed exactly, renders the remaining five hundred pages meaningless.

Energumen. (En-er-<u>gyoo</u>-men) **n**. *A fanatical enthusiast*. Anyone to whom this description applies in the context of the work of Tracey Emin should be kept away from the knife drawer.

Enfelon. (En-<u>fe</u>-lon) **vt**. *To infuriate*. Great enjoyment can be derived, at no expense, by engaging in a bit of enfeloning now and then. Try this out, for example. When you are in a supermarket at a particularly busy time, and you have a longish queue behind you at the checkout, take your time filling your bags with the stuff that is passed to you by the checkout girl. Then empty one of the bags completely and refill it very carefully. Ask the checkout girl at least three times how much it all costs, then query the price of an item lying at the bottom of one of the bags. Get it out and have it checked. Refill the bag. Fish around in your pockets, pulling your wallet out of the last pocket you check. Open it very slowly and choose a credit card. Hand it to the checkout girl, then change your mind and ask for it back. Give her another card. Make sure that this one has expired, so that you have to go through all your pockets again to find some cash. Pull out a handful of loose change. Pay the exact amount, using coins of the smallest possible denomination, pretending that you are short-sighted and can't see them very well. Get the amount wrong a couple of times so that you have to start all over again. Put the receipt into your wallet (found only after going through your pockets several times) and put your wallet back into your pocket, before gathering up your carrier bags and slowly moving off. Drop one, or preferably two, bags before you clear the checkout; tell the checkout girl you have a bad back and ask her to call someone to help you pick it all up. That done, walk briskly and cheerily from the shop.

Enlimn. (En-<u>lim</u>) **vt**. *To paint something using bright colours.*
What Barbara Cartland did, with terrifying effect.

Enneatic. (E-nee-a-tik) **a**. *Occurring once in nine times.*

> A cat, with a smile quite superior,
> Said, 'Dogs, and such like, are inferior.
> I find it quite fine
> That of lives I've got nine.
> In fact, there are few things much eerier.'
>
> As he leapt from a window exterior,
> You never saw anyone cheerier.
> On the way down, a bat
> Said, 'But you're not a cat.
> You're a mammal from northern Nigeria.'
>
> (Now mammals from northern Nigeria
> Are sold by a crook from Liberia.
> As 'cats' they're imported
> And then they're transported
> To pet shops with motives ulterior.)
>
> This news was received with hysteria;
> But amongst the defining criteria
> Of African creatures
> There quite often features
> A very elastic posterior.

> *The mammal from northern Nigeria,*
> *Having bounced, said in tones a bit wearier,*
> *'Survival like that*
> *Means I must be a cat,'*
> *Then died – killed by toxic bacteria.*

Enoptromancy. (En-<u>op</u>-troe-man-see) **n**. *Divination by the use of mirrors*. A technique the Meteorological Office should give a go. It couldn't be worse than using the present technology, and would certainly be considerably cheaper.

Enseam. (En-<u>seem</u>) **vt**. *To stitch up*. As used when referring to a murder investigation when there is someone who lives within ten miles of the crime scene and to whom the label of 'loner' can be attached.

Ensear. (En-<u>seer</u>) **vi**. *To dry up*. It was the well-known geriatrician Dr W. J. Smythies who first noted that the total quantity of fluid excreted by an individual over a 24-hour period remained roughly constant throughout life. He showed that when the process of ageing led to fluid output by one route ensearing, output by another route automatically increased by way of compensation, and vice versa. As Smythies succinctly expressed his Law of Excretory Constancy:

In old age, what doesn't dry up, leaks.

W. James Smythies
Growing Old Gracefully? Forget It (1978)

Epalpebrate. (Ee-<u>pal</u>-pi-br't) **a**. *Lacking eyebrows*. A descriptive term that one always looks forward to applying to the individual (usually, in my experience, a short man with a moustache and mad eyes) who insists that he is the only one responsible enough to light the fireworks on Bonfire Night.

Ephialtes. (E-fee-<u>al</u>-teez) **n**. *A nightmare*. Particularly one in which the horror is extreme, causing one to wake up screaming and drenched with sweat (as, for example, dreaming that one is trapped in a lift with an American).

Epiky. (<u>E</u>-pi-kee) **n**. *Reasonableness*. The now-abandoned principle of the British legal system, which once ensured that compensation payments were not awarded to those injured as a consequence of their doing something suggestive of serious intellectual impairment.

Eremite. (<u>E</u>-re-miyt) **n**. *A recluse*. One who adopts a lifestyle that could be highly recommended to socially prominent individuals given to airing their opinions in public.

Eristic. (E-<u>ri</u>-stik) **a**. *Controversial*. I would hope that the term 'eristic,' used to describe an idea or opinion which rests upon little or no evidence, may eventually come to replace the much misused word 'controversial,' the latter being too often applied inappropriately to notions which are informed but unconventional. An informed view is controversial only to a person who is either uninformed or misinformed. This is worth bearing in mind when the presenter of an early-morning radio programme dealing with topical affairs describes an issue as being 'controversial.'

Errable. (E̲-ra-b'l) **a**. *Fallible.*

> *Pope Percival the First said, 'I'm infallible*
> *And everything I tell you must be true.*
> *There's an elephant that flies;*
> *All the stars are apple pies;*
> *And wine is made from Silvikrin shampoo.'*
>
> *The Cardinals, aghast, said, 'Popes are errable!'*
> *But Percival the First said, 'No they're not.*
> *I've a direct line to God*
> *(I'm the Pope, so that's not odd),*
> *And when it comes to knowledge, God's red hot.'*
>
> *The Cardinals all muttered, 'This is terrible!*
> *He's mad, and must be silenced double-quick.*
> *If he's not, he'll just besmirch*
> *Our Holy Roman Church.*
> *Let's tell the world that Percival is sick!'*
>
> *They slipped the Pope a poison quite comestible.*
> *Soon Percival the First was lying dead.*
> *Then the heavens split apart,*
> *And God boomed, 'That wasn't smart.'*
> *How they wished that they'd believed what Percy said.*

Erubescence. (E-roo-be̲-s'ns) **n**. *Blushing.* A reaction to the recognition that one has committed a serious social solecism, and that the whole world knows and is talking about it. The physiological basis of this reaction appears, however, to be lacking amongst those who charge excessively for speaking at charity fund-raising events.

Erugate. (E̲-roo-gaet) **vt**. *To smooth out wrinkles*. A term that is useful in the cosmetics industry in the sense of 'to rejuvenate the skin,' and also in the building trade to mean 'to fill old cracks with plaster.'

Esculent. (E̲s-kyoo-l'nt) **a**. *Edible*.

> *It's really quite incredible*
> *What Frenchmen think is edible.*
> *They have a simple rule*
> *They believe is rather cool:*
> *It moves? Then you can eat it;*
> *It's still? Then first you heat it.*
> *Or so a Frenchman said;*
> *But after dinner he was dead.*

Esemplastic. (E-sem-pla̲-stik) **a**. *Unifying*. A description that politicians use when cobbling together a single country out of two or more geographical regions (however this may come about – as a result of conquest, treaty or, as in the case of Iraq, sheer ineptitude and an inability to foresee the blindingly obvious consequences). When the populations of the separate regions differ in language, customs, religion or cultural values, and have, as a consequence, a sense of nationhood in their own right, there is an inevitable – and therefore entirely predictable (except, of course, to politicians) – tendency for such a country to break up again. What politicians seem unable to grasp is that nationalism is a force of nature, and that stopping it is like pushing water back up a tap.

Esperanto. (E-sper-<u>ran</u>-toe) **n**. *The international language invented by Dr L. L. Zamenhof.* Yes, I know that this is not a word that ever really became lost, but I include it because I feel that its use could profitably be extended to cover more or less any good idea that is treated with the contempt that doddypolls *(q.v.)* think it deserves.

Essera. (<u>E</u>-ser-ra) **n**. *A form of nettle rash.* Reserved for the unpleasant condition brought on by thinking about truly appalling people, such as those who quote John Lennon, willingly eat prawn cocktail, or are learning Cornish.

Estrepement. (E-<u>streep</u>-m'nt) **n**. *The laying waste of land.* The official name for the UK government's agricultural policy. *(See also **Crool** and **Pabulous**.)*

Estuosity. (E-styoo-<u>o</u>-si-tee) **n**. *A state of heatedness.* Such as the effect produced in motorists confronted by traffic lights on all roads leading on to a roundabout, when, as all rational, sentient beings know, the roundabout was put there in the first place to eliminate the need for traffic lights.

Ethician. (E-<u>thi</u>-sh'n) **n**. *An expert on ethics*. A person who says that anything they don't personally like or agree with 'raises serious ethical issues.'

Eudæmony. (*Y*oo-<u>de</u>-mo-nee, *or Y*oo-<u>dee</u>-mo-nee) **n**. *A state of happy prosperity*. The popularity of the lottery depends upon the belief that wealth, particulary when out of all proportion to the effort expended in its acquisition, is essential for happiness. If those holding such a view were not entirely impervious to reason, their attachment to the lottery could be dispelled by suggesting that they take a good look at the royal families of the world.

Euge. (*Y*ooj) **excl**. *Well done!* What back-slapping MPs say to each other after voting for further benefits to be added to their already gold-plated pension scheme. The word may also be used adjectivally to describe the pension payments they may expect to receive.

Eunomy. (*Y*oo-no-mee) **n**. *The state achieved when a well-conceived law is also well administered*. Or when an iceberg spontaneously combusts.

Euplastic. (*Y*oo-<u>pla</u>-stik) **a**. *Readily shaped or moulded*. A term that may be applied to ethical principles when self-interest, and particularly cash, is involved. (*See also* **Ethician**.)

Eutaxy. (*Y*oo-tak-see) **n**. *A state of good order*. What, according to a leaked e-mail from the Home Office to the Prime

Minister, only a nuclear strike could produce in Toxteth.

Eventeration. (Ee-ven-ter-<u>rae</u>-sh'n) **n**. *Disembowelment*. A sequel to hanging and a prelude to quartering, eventeration represents an unpleasant interlude between two ghastly events. It was in this figurative sense that the word was used by the historian Graham Purley, in *England, Poor England* (1977), to refer to the Regency period in English history.

Evigilation. (Ee-vi-ji-<u>lae</u>-sh'n) **n**. *An awakening*. If the attack on the Twin Towers was, as described at the time, America's evigilation call, the subsequent decisions to invade Iraq and Afghanistan were certainly the equivalent of hitting the snooze button.

Evite. (<u>Ee</u>-viyt) **n**. *A female wearing few clothes*. More or less any female in more or less any UK town centre after eleven o'clock at night – even, for God's sake, when it's snowing.

Exarate. (<u>Ek</u>-sa-raet) **vt**. *To make a written note*. The primary function of a nurse in an NHS hospital.

Exosculation. (Eks-os-kyoo-<u>lae</u>-sh'n) **n**. *A heartfelt kiss*. As, for example, administered by unsuccessful Oscar nominees to the Oscar winner.

Exust. (Ek-<u>sust</u>) **vt**. *To burn*. An action to be deplored as cultural vandalism when done to books – except novels by Jilly Cooper, in which case there ought to be grants given for it.

F

Facetiæ. (Fa-<u>see</u>-shi-ee) **n**. *Humorous writings*. When faced with someone who is particularly smug about their forthcoming holiday on a sun-drenched Pacific island, you should advise them to take some light, humorous reading with them, in case (as you assure them is highly likely) there are no bookshops to be found on their island. Press upon them your copy of the *Collected Plays of Ibsen* and anything you can lay your hands on by Solzhenitsyn.

Facient. (<u>Fa</u>-sh'nt) **n**. *A doer*. One who makes an essential contribution to the wealth of a nation, as distinct from someone who receives a seven-figure bonus for fouling up the international economy by lending that wealth to people who haven't a dog's chance of ever paying it back. *(See also **Latrociny**.)*

Facinorous. (Fa-<u>si</u>-nor-r's) **a**. *Exceptionally wicked*. As, for example, any pudding prepared by Duncan, chef at the Wolf House Gallery Restaurant in Silverdale.

Facund. (<u>Fa</u>-kund) **a**. *Eloquent*. A quality which, when encountered, should make one dive for cover, or at the very least check that one's gun is loaded. Honest, sincere, considered, logical, intelligent, clear-sighted: an eloquent speaker may be all of these things – or none. *(See also **Chrysostomic**.)*

Faitour. (<u>Fae</u>-ter) **n**. *A cheat who pretends to be able to see into the future.* May now be used to mean 'a financial adviser.' The term is also useful in the north-west of England to refer to weather forecasters.

Famulus. (<u>Fa</u>-myoo-lus) **n**. *Servant to a scholar.* A word no longer required in the UK, though not because of any shortage of servants.

Fangle. (<u>Fan</u>-g'l) **n**. *A silly contraption.*

> The word 'fangle' came originally from the name of the nineteenth-century inventor Arthur Fangle (1802–1851), who designed over four hundred labour-saving devices. Fangle was delighted when his large steam-powered machine for grooming small dogs was selected for the Great Exhibition in 1851, believing that this recognition of his talents would inevitably herald the commercial success that had so far eluded any of his inventions. Two weeks into the Exhibition, however, a design fault in the dog-grooming machine's combustion chamber caused a violent explosion, killing Fangle outright. Lady Uppingham's pug Ernest, who was inside the machine at the time, was never found.
>
> Sidney Orpington
> *Words the Victorians Gave Us* (1998)

Fantast. (<u>Fan</u>-tast) **n**. *A visionary*. What all politicians would like to be thought of as being – and what, indeed, in the medical sense, most of them appear to be.

Fardel. (<u>Far</u>-d'l) **n**. *A burden of sin*. That which some believe can be shed by confession. This may explain why a number of prominent people, quite late in life, convert to Roman Catholicism, without, one suspects, having checked the small print, which would have revealed a sentence or two about repentance also being necessary. *(See also **Remord**.)*

Farouche. (Fa-<u>roosh</u>) **a**. *Having a sullen and repellent manner*. Once a requirement for being employed to serve food in UK motorway service stations, but a term that may not find a great deal of use now that the Poles and Lithuanians are getting the jobs.

Fashious. (<u>Fa</u>-sh's) **a**. *Tiresome*. A term that is applied by the people of Europe to any Directive issued by the European Commission (except by the Italians, who never read them). *(See also **Anenterous** and **Aporrhœa**.)*

Fastidium. (Fa-<u>sti</u>-dee-um) **n**. *Disgust*.

> *I'm very bold when faced with mould,*
> *And I can stand* Clostridium,
> *But when I see a KFC*
> *I throw up in fastidium.*

Featous. (<u>Fee</u>-t's) **a**. *Wrought in an artistic manner*. Once used to describe the work of Michelangelo, Renoir and Constable, but now applicable to more or less anything left strewn about on Tracey Emin's floor.

Fedity. (<u>Fe</u>-di-tee) **n**. *Loathsome practice*. There being none greater than the addition of lemonade to a single malt.

Femalist. (<u>Fee</u>-ma-list) **n**. *A person who is pro-female*. To be distinguished from a feminist (who is merely anti-male).

Fen. (Fen) **vt**. *To forbid*. That is, to infringe another person's fundamental human right to do whatever, wherever, whenever, and to whomever they want.

Fere. (Feer) **n**. *A mate*.

> *Monty Jarvis was a sporty sort of chap,*
> *With a very healthy golfing handicap.*
> *The kind of guy who thinks he's heaven's gift,*
> *And whose homing-in on girls is pretty swift.*
> *When he spotted Wendy Henderson, he said,*
> *'Would you like to join me, darling, in my bed?*
> *I'm quite sure that you'd find happiness, my dear,*
> *If only you'd consent to be my fere.'*
> *Wendy laughed, and gave her answer, loud and clear.*
> *'Sleep with you, you smarmy crocodile? No fear.'*

Ferity. (<u>Fe</u>-ri-tee) **n**. *Barbarity*. This is potentially a most versatile word which could, for example, be applied to whaling, dog fighting, badger baiting, or spending any portion of the public libraries' budget on computers.

Ferly. (<u>Fer</u>-lee) **a**. *Wonderfully strange*. A term usefully and accurately applied to the thought processes of those who, having been shown a list of those selected to be judges for the Man Booker Prize, continue to take the thing seriously. *(See also **Clamjamphrie**.)*

Fictile. (<u>Fik</u>-tiyl) **a**. *Capable of being shaped or moulded*. A quality which the term 'reserves of oil' confers upon an otherwise inflexible foreign policy. *(See also **Euplastic**.)*

Fifish. (<u>Fiy</u>-fish) **a**. *Deranged*. Originally used exclusively in relation to the people of the county of Fife, this term may now be extended to include those who describe public libraries as 'dynamic social spaces,' and not simply as places where books are to be found.

Fike. (Fiyk) **vi**. *To fidget*. An intense urge to fike occurs two minutes into the first act of *Peter Grimes* and grows inexorably as the opera continues. The condition can be moderately alleviated by immoderate quantities of gin. *(See also **Absonous**, **Findy** and **Hoppestere**.)*

Findy. (<u>Fin</u>-dee) **a**. *Solid and weighty*. As, for example, an object which, if it had been applied early enough to Benjamin Britten's head, could have forestalled many an addiction to gin. *(See also **Absonous**, **Fike** and **Hoppestere**.)*

Finew. (<u>Fin</u>-yoo) **n**. *Mouldiness*. That which on bread revolts, but on cheese delights – hence the potential figurative use of the term to mean something demonstrating context-specific attractiveness. Thus, one might say, 'Although the vulgarity of his language had closed many a door against him in his search for employment, it eventually turned out to be a finew, being the deciding factor in his being chosen to host a TV chat show.'

Fitten. (<u>Fi</u>-t'n) **n**. *A lie*. Also, a general term for the words a politician learns before he can say 'Mummy.'

Fizgig. (<u>Fiz</u>-gig) **n**. *A frivolous and fun-loving female*. If also an Evite *(q.v.)*, this is certainly the one to invite.

Flagitious. (Fla-<u>ji</u>-sh's) **a**. *Guilty of an atrocious crime*. One can imagine that an infinitely compassionate and loving God would be prepared to forgive the majority of those guilty of the most foul and heinous deeds. There are, however, some who commit crimes so atrocious that they will surely, and deservedly, burn in the everlasting flames of Hell. I speak, of course, of those who made the decision to abandon the teaching of classical languages in our schools, those found in possession of a computer game, those who deny the superiority of Lancashire Creamy Mild over all other cheeses, and *particularly* those who put brown bread in bread-and-butter pudding.

Flam. (Flam) **n**. *A fabrication*. A straight transliteration of the Russian word 'флам,' meaning 'a free and fair, democratically conducted election.'

Fleer. (Fleer) **vi**. *To smile contemptuously*. An involuntary reaction to the outcome of British general elections in which the result in marginal constituencies is determined by postal votes. *(See also* **Obreption**.*)*

Flirtigig. (Fler-ti-gig) **n**. *A giddy female*. A fizgig *(q.v.)* on Buck's Fizz.

Flite. (Fliyt) **vt**. *To scold*. What, according to historical sources, parents used to do to their children to curb unruly behaviour, though, according to Blubell Scree in *How to Beg to Your Child* (2007), it is now believed by child-rearing experts that the true meaning of 'flite' must have been 'to negotiate.'

Flitty. (Fli-tee) **a**. *Unstable*. As in the commonly used phrase 'as flitty as a Turner Prize judge.' *(See also* **Amenty**.*)*

Flotten. (Flo-t'n) **a**. *Skimmed*. The policies and practices of the major supermarket chains mean that 'flotten' may now be applied equally to milk and the farmers who produce it. In similar vein, J. Frederick Neilson (in *The Democracy Hypocrisy*, 2003) used the term substantively to mean 'the electorate.'

Flump. (Flump) **vi**. *To fall heavily with a dull thud*. A word that would cause jubilation were it to appear in the same news report (and, with any luck, in the same sentence) as 'Director General of the BBC' and 'iron bar.' *(See also **Fnese** and **Leam**.)*

Fnese. (Fneez) **vi**. *To puff and snort*. The inevitable response of anyone listening to the BBC Director General's justification for the way in which the Corporation spends its licence fee income. *(See also **Flump** and **Leam**.)*

Fogger. (<u>Fo</u>-ger) **n**. *A lawyer given to underhand practices*. Now that our political masters have not only arranged things so that virtually anything we do is a criminal offence, but have also started to erode our rights to trial by jury, one can't help thinking that recourse to the services of a fogger is the best (and probably the only) chance one has of keeping out of jail.

Foleye. (Fo-<u>lee</u>) **vi**. *To play the fool*. According to Wilberforce Stannard in *Stannard's Guide to Parliamentary Procedures* (1929), 'foleye' has its origins in the Norman French 'foilyer' ('to make a pronouncement') and was once commonly used in the specific sense of 'to make a speech in the House of Commons.' It is not known how it came subsequently to carry the connotation of foolishness.

Fon. (Fon) **vi**. *To become foolishly infatuated*. This was only ever used in the form of 'fonned.'

> *'Ah, woe!' the maid, despairing, wept.*
> *'Of me he was but fond.*
> *Oh, why so little did he feel*
> *When I of him was fonned?'*

Foozle. (<u>Foo</u>-z'l) **vt**. *To make a total mess of something*. A word that is now used only when talking of successive ministers responsible for Education, Health, Agriculture, Trade, Finance, Culture, Overseas Development, Employment etc.

Fopdoodle. (<u>Fop</u>-doo-d'l) **n**. *A simpleton*. A term applied primarily to someone who foozles *(see* **Foozle***)*. Thus the members of the Cabinet may be described as foozling fopdoodles.

Fordwine. (For-<u>dwiyn</u>) **v**. *To wither away*.

> *That which falls into disuse will surely fordwine. If it be*
> *an instrument of harm, then we may rejoice; but if it be the*
> *proper and seemly use of language, then should we put on*
> *the dark attire of mourning and lamentation.*
>
> Sir Elquin Marples
> *Sic Transit Lingua* (1813)

Fossulate. (<u>Fos</u>-yoo-l't) **a**. *Having a series of long grooves*. The only known example of the use of this word in recent years was by the film critic and professional harridan Shirley Dalrymple, in reference to Mariella Kroop, vampish star of some thirty epic films spanning almost half a century. In 2002, in her weekly column in *Film and Filmgoers*, Dalrymple wrote that:

> *If Miss Kroop were to remove the bulldog clip from the back of her head, her face would become immediately and dramatically fossulate.*

As the word 'fossulate' appeared in no American dictionary, Miss Kroop's subsequent libel action was dismissed, and costs were awarded to Dalrymple.

Fougue. (Foog) **n**. *Impetuosity*. That which the old, on the basis of their own experience, attempt to curb in the young. The attempt fortunately not succeeding, the young are thus permitted to gain the experience on which to base their own future pointless attempts to curb fougue in their own children. And so ad infinitum.

Frab. (Frab) **vi**. *To worry*. Like the attempt to curb fougue *(q.v.)*, frabbing is another ultimately pointless piece of behaviour on the part of the old towards the young.

Fragor. (<u>Fra</u>-gor) **n**. *A loud crash*. The inevitable consequence of giving a two-year-old free run of the house, or politicians free run of a country.

Frape. (Fraep) **n**. *A rabble*. What politicians suspect the people to be, but what the people know politicians to be.

Frim. (Frim) **a**. *Plump and juicy*. Things really don't get much better than when a flirtigig *(q.v.)* is frim, unless, of course, she's an Evite *(q.v.)* as well.

Frounce. (Frowns) **n**. *Duplicity*.

> *If frounce did not exist, it would be necessary to invent it — if, that is, we wished not to put the whole of the diplomatic corps out of work.*
>
> Sir Ronald Hogan
> (British Consul, Monteverde, Uruguay, 1955–1969)
> *The Diplomatic Corpse* (1972)

Fubsy. (<u>Fub</u>-see) **a**. *Squat and fat*. In the late 1960s, Marigold Fubsy, a short but grossly obese fashion designer, produced a range of clothes based on her own body measurements. Although at that time they did not sell at all well, clothes bearing the Fubsy label have recently become much in demand, especially in the UK teenage market.

Fuff. (Fuf) **n**. *A whiff*. As of the heavily perfumed slipstream of a frim *(q.v.)* flirtigig *(q.v.)* at full throttle.

Fustigate. (<u>Fu</u>-sti-gaet) **vt**. *To beat or cudgel*. A term used to describe what happens after a Yemeni policeman says, 'Perhaps you'd be kind enough to accompany us to the station, sir. Nothing to worry about – just a minor routine enquiry.'

Fustilugs. (<u>Fus</u>-ti-lugz) **n**. *A gross and corpulent woman*. An unfortunate woman with an abnormally low metabolic rate, an underfunctioning thyroid, an allergic response to food with a 'low carbohydrate density,' and a handbag containing eighty-five thousand calories.

G

Gabber. (<u>Ga</u>-ber) **n**. *One who deceives*. Also showing resurgence as a term for the person who arranges for the words 'Number One International Bestseller' to be printed on a book's cover before the book has been seen by anyone outside the publisher's office (and often before it has been written).

Gadling. (<u>Gad</u>-ling) **n**. *A wandering rogue*. Applicable specifically to ex-presidents or ex-prime ministers, and to the spouses of either, who drift from one after-dinner speaking engagement to another. There are now so many gadlings travelling around that airlines are sometimes unable to cope without laying on more aircraft. The broadcaster Philip Brook commented (28 October 2007) that he would be happy to organize a cull if someone could come up with a gadling gun.

Galimatias. (Ga-li-<u>mae</u>-sh's) **n**. *Gibberish*. A rare word, of obscure origin, which could now be used to mean 'an explanation of what any exhibit in Tate Modern represents.'

Galp. (Galp) **vi**. *To gape, yawn or vomit.* Any or all of which are appropriate responses to conceptual art. *(See also **Gane** and **Gaure**.)*

Gane. (Gaen) **vi**. *To open the mouth wide.* As when faced with pretentiousness, in whatever form it may take.

> 'The brick that stands upon the floor
> Is peace and love.
> The broken saw
> Is war.'
> The artist pointed to a cup
> 'And that's the door
> To hell.'
> 'Why are they stuck together, then?'
> A man enquired.
> 'Because they tell
> A unitary story, though they stand apart
> As well.'
> 'Why did you paint them green?'
> 'The sky is green with envy.'
> 'That's something that I've never seen.'
> 'Perhaps you never look,'
> The Artist said.
> Then added, 'Always try
> To think in squares.
> I feel that there's
> So much to gain.'

> *He looked at those to whom he spoke.*
> *'Why do you gane?'*
> *He asked.*

Gar. (Gar) **vt**. *To make*. Although this and its synonyms have become obsolete in the English language, 'gar' has recently been incorporated into Mandarin and Cantonese.

Garget. (<u>Gar</u>-get) **n**. *The throat*. Also refers to the flexible tube down which European legislation travels under pressure.

Gaure. (Gowr) **vi**. *To gape*. As, for example, to respond appropriately to someone who refers to the craftsmanship of Damien Hirst. *(See also **Galp** and **Gane**.)*

Gibeonite. (<u>Gi</u>-bee-o-niyt) **n**. *A hard worker*. In the Book of Ezriel it is recounted how the attachment of the Gibeonites to wealth and worldly goods so offended God that he loosed a plague of flies upon them, which drove them from their land and into the land of the Edreonites. There they became shopkeepers and merchants, working so hard that they soon became rich again. God told the prophet Nemeziah to command his people to abandon their commercial enterprises and lead a more holy life. The Gibeonites, however, were doing nicely, thank you very much, and told Nemeziah to take a walk. Angered by this, God caused the Edreonites to drive the Gibeonites into the land of the Lemites who, not being enamoured of hard work themselves (and being, into the bargain, financially rather naive), were completely unprepared for what hit them. In a dream, God told Nemeziah that it was clearly inevitable that the hard-working Gibeonites would bring upon themselves the curse of riches in whatever land they might reside, and that, as far as he was concerned, from now on they could go hang. This appears to be the only occasion in the Old Testament when God threw in the towel.

Gim. (Jim) **a**. *Of smart appearance*. According to Lancashire folklore, Gim was a woodland sprite who, taking pity on the people of the county because of the ragged and untidy clothes they wore, magically transformed their garments into ones that were smart as new. The King of the Sprites, however, was angry when he learned of this, and accused Gim of upsetting the natural order of things. Gim was banished from Lancashire, never to return.

Gleek. (Gleek) **n**. *A trinity*.

> *Far easier it is to grasp*
> *The concept of infinity*
> *Than understand the mystery*
> *That is the Holy Trinity.*
>
> *I've tried to fathom what it means,*
> *But 'Three-in-One,' and 'One-in-Three,'*
> *My intellect just cannot grasp.*
> *It really is all Gleek to me.*

Gleet. (Gleet) **vi**. *To produce something disagreeable.* A word that is most commonly used as the gerund, as, for example, in the resignation of Cardinal Ophithanios of Heraklion in 1921. Speaking in English when addressing the Vatican Council, Cardinal Ophithanios said:

> *I stand before you, Holy Father and my Lord Cardinals, a changed man. I have reflected long and have concluded that this earthly life is all too brief and fleeting, and that I cannot afford to spend the few short years that are left to me in tending my flock.*
>
> *I am beset by those (they are many) who whine and complain and prostrate themselves before even the smallest difficulty or inconvenience placed before them by the vagaries of life.*
>
> *I hereby resign from the Cardinalate because I no longer hear the bleating of lambs who have strayed from the path, but only the gleeting of those who would be too feckless to follow it, even if led by rings in their noses.*

> Pietro Luosi
> *Life and Times of Ophithanios* (1980)

Gleg. (Gleg) **a**. *Quick to understand.* Why is it, one wonders, that government ministers who blame the incompetence of junior civil servants for what are obviously spectactular foul-ups caused by the government's failure to think things through, are never gleg that the electorate *is? (See also* **Yarely**.*)*

Gliff. (Glif) **n**. *A passing glance*. Rather more than needs to be accorded to the news-sheets circulated to all households by city and county councils at an annual cost that could keep at least two branch libraries open. *(See also **Laniate**.)*

Glump. (Glump) **n**. *A sulky individual*. What one used to be taught at school *not* to be after losing a race, a game of rugby or a cricket match. Professional footballers evidently did not attend that kind of school. *(See also **Mammothrept**.)*

Gnomology. (Noe-<u>mo</u>-lo-jee) **n**. *A collection of moral precepts*. Specifically, those dealing with improper behaviour towards garden ornaments.

Gobemouche. (<u>Go</u>-be-moosh, *or* <u>Goe</u>-be-moosh) **n**. *A person who believes all news*. A term that is rather more polite than telling someone they have the IQ of a toothbrush.

Goodlihead. (<u>Gud</u>-lee-hed) **n**. *Excellence*.

EDUCATION MINISTER: This year, 79.3% of all those taking A-level examinations achieved a grade which equates with excellence.

DR WELLS: And does that meet the government's target, Minister?

EDUCATION MINISTER: By no means. Not until, by further reforming the curriculum, we can report that excellence has been achieved by 100% of pupils.

DR WELLS: So that excellence will be the norm?

EDUCATION MINISTER: Exactly!

DR WELLS: The norm, Minister, is also referred to as the average.

EDUCATION MINISTER: I don't follow you, Dr Wells.

DR WELLS: It's simply this, Minister: your 'reforms' to the curriculum will, if they work to plan, ensure that the achievement of all pupils is average, and that none, therefore, can be regarded as attaining excellence.

EDUCATION MINISTER: That's mere sophistry, Dr Wells.

DR WELLS: Not mere sophistry, Minister – mere statistics.

> Transcript of a meeting between Dr N. H. Wells of the Department of Education, University of Knightsbridge, and George Booting MP, Minister of Education
> 15 November 2007

Gorbelly. (<u>Gor</u>-be-lee) **n**. *A corpulent person*. In the UK, this is now used only in the compound term 'gorbelly-saw,' a particularly powerful form of chainsaw used by undertakers to joint corpses so as to fit them into two or more coffins of a size that won't wedge the crematorium furnace doors open.

Grandevous. (Gran-<u>dee</u>-v's) **a**. *Old*. Describes the point at which the age of one's body and the age that one feels finally become one and the same.

Grassant. (<u>Gra</u>-s*n) **a**. *Lying in wait, with evil intent.*

> *The highwayman, as dusk descends,*
> *Observes the coach* en passant.
> *'There's gold and silver to be had!'*
> *Declares the villain, grassant.*

Groof. (Groof) **a**. *Face downwards*. The preferred orientation, usually in the vicinity of a gutter, adopted by a high proportion of British visitors to Marbella.

Grubble. (<u>Gru</u>-b'l) **vi/vt**. *To grope*. It has been suggested to me by Mr Julian Dorning, CEO of Dorning Industries plc, that this word might usefully be used in large commercial companies to mean 'to attend the company's Christmas party,' though I remain unclear as to the reasoning behind the proposal.

Gular. (<u>Gyoo</u>-lar) **a**. *Passionate about good food*. This may also be used to describe the mental anguish which arises if one is obliged to spend a week in Gateshead.

Gustless. (<u>Gust</u>-l's) **a**. *Tasteless*. The original recipe for what is now called simply 'Yorkshire pudding' appeared in *Cookynge For Laydeys* (1597) by Lady Anne Blacklocke, where its full title was given as 'Yorkishe, or Gustlesse, Puddynge.'

Guttatim. (Gu-<u>tae</u>-tim) **adv**. *Drop by drop*. Lady Anne Blacklocke (1597) stipulated that gravy should be poured onto Yorkshire pudding 'guttatim.' This has always puzzled culinary experts because the viscosity of gravy as made in Yorkshire precludes its being poured from anything onto anything. *(See also* **Gustless***.)*

Gyromancy. (J̲iy-roe-man-see) **n**. *Divination by going round in circles.* The best way to understand what gyromancy involves is to telephone the Department of Business, Enterprise and Regulatory Reform and ask for clarification of the double taxation arrangements between the UK and Spain. After being passed to the fifteenth person, you will be in a position to predict with confidence that the future will not be characterized by any sense of enlightenment, satisfaction or accomplishment.

Gyte. (Giyt) **a**. *Off one's head*. This comes from the name of Maureen Gyte, an Irish contralto who gave a private recital of songs in the Irish language before Prime Minister Margaret Thatcher and Mikhail Gorbachev on the occasion of the latter's first official visit to London. The following day it was learned that Miss Gyte had been discharged from a private psychiatric clinic in Cork only a week previously; moreover, it appeared that the lyrics of all the songs in her recital had been written by her and were almost unbelievably obscene. A month later, after trying to set fire to the Book of Kells in Trinity College library, Miss Gyte was admitted to the Dublin Psychiatric Institute and remained there until her death in 2001.

H

Hake. (Haek) **vt**. *To pester*. Haking, done well and by an expert, is an art form.

> *Oh, are we there yet, Dad? Why not?*
> *How far is there to go?*
> *I want to wee. I'm feeling sick.*
> *I've got a poorly toe.*
> *Ow! Sally's hitting me again.*
> *She's opening the door.*
> *Dad, can I wind the window down?*
> *Look, Sally's on the floor.*
> *She's eating something sticky, Dad.*
> *Dad, can I have a drink?*
> *Dad, Dad, I left the gerbil out;*
> *I think he's in the sink.*
> *D'you think he'll eat the gingerbread*
> *That Mum left on a plate?*
> *Perhaps the dog will get him first.*
> *Hey, Dad, will we be late?*
> *Dad, Sally's got a great big knife.*

Oh, yuk! That looks like blood.
I think she's cut a finger off —
She told me that she would.
Dad, can I have her finger, Dad?
Oh, cripes! It isn't that!
It's something long and furry, Dad.
I think she's got the cat.
She's never liked its tail, you know.
Dad, can I have a rat?
Samantha Lee has five of them.
Dad, Sally's got my hat.
She's cut a great big hole in it.
Oh, Dad! That hat was new!
Will Grandpa mend my bicycle?
Dad, is the Bible true?
Oh, Dad, I'm feeling really *bored.*
My seat belt's come undone.
What's that you're pointing at your head?
Hey, Dad, is that a gun?
What's that *for, Dad? Dad, is it real?*
D'you keep it in the car?
Joe Green has got a crossbow, Dad.
I'm fed up! Is it far?

Bang.

Haply. (Hap-lee) **adv**. *By accident.* The only reason for visiting Goole.

Hardiesse. (Har-dee-<u>es</u>) **n**. *Boldness*. Useful when referring to someone who chooses to stick his head out of a window in Kabul, Beirut, Baghdad, Harare, the Bronx, Rangoon or Liverpool.

Harmans. (<u>Har</u>-manz) **n**. *The stocks*. What an enlightened government would reintroduce for the incorrect use of 'enormity.'

Hastif. (<u>Ha</u>-stif) **a**. *Precipitate*. A useful word to use when a woman takes less than two hours to buy an item of clothing.

Haught. (Hort) **a**. *High in one's own estimation*. That personal characteristic which makes someone simultaneously obnoxious and, unfortunately, most unlikely to jump off a cliff. Also, a necessary attribute of one seeking appointment to public office, but which, in any well-designed social system, would be an absolute disbarment from doing so.

Haussmannize. (<u>Hows</u>-ma-niyz) **vt**. *To dismantle, and then reconstruct on more formal lines*. Fortunately done in Paris, but even more fortunately not done in Rome, thereby demonstrating – to the astonishment of architects – the nonuniversality of architectural dicta.

Haviours. (<u>Hae</u>-vy'z) **n**. *Good manners*. A word that may usefully be generalized to mean anything the necessity for which becomes obvious only when it is absent, and encompasses the concepts of 'truthfulness,' 'politeness,' 'attentiveness,' 'courtesy,' 'consideration for others' and 'the correct use of the apostrophe.'

Hawm. (Horm) **vi**. *To make awkward and ugly movements*. Useful as a technical term in modern dance choreography.

Hawse. (Horz) **vt**. *To treat someone, without objective justification, as being more distinguished than others, particularly in terms of intellect and matters of taste*. If hawsing did not exist, it is doubtful whether the institution of monarchy would last more than a week. *Rex deus est. (See also* **Reptation***.)*

Heaume. (Hoem) **n**. *A large helmet reaching almost to the shoulders*. As, for example, the headgear that an American football player wears, but a rugby player refuses to wear, because neither wishes to be seen dead in it.

Heavisome. (He-vi-s'm) **a**. *Mildly depressed*. A state of mind into which one slips after trying to find a bookshop selling any books that one has not already seen in all the other bookshops (and selling at least one book that one feels like reading).

Hebetate. (He-bi-t't) **a**. *Lacking a point*. A word that would never be used by those modern educationalists who are able to see (though no-one else can) the point of studying, at secondary-school level, subjects such as psychology, sociology, modern dance, and media studies.

Heeze. (Heez) **vt**. *To hoist*. A verb that one fears may, in one's own case, some day be paired with 'bath' and 'lavatory.'

Helmage. (<u>Hel</u>-mij) **n**. *Guidance*. A term that, having slid into abeyance, seems doomed to remain there, because guidance – whatever word one uses for it – may no longer be offered in the UK by anyone to anyone about anything, for fear of litigation.

Henotic. (He-<u>no</u>-tik) **a**. *Reconciliatory*. This, together with 'compassionate,' 'forgiving' and 'tolerant,' is ascribed by adherents of every religion to the attitude that their God takes towards the world, its peoples and other religions – an attitude which, curiously, they do not feel it worthwhile to adopt themselves.

Hern. (Hern) **n**. *A corner*. That into which an interviewer worth his salt manages to drive an interviewee who holds strong and inflexible views about something or other. Done with skill, herning can be highly instructive, though when the interviewee is a politician it is far too easily and quickly accomplished to offer much in the way of entertainment.

Hery. (<u>Heer</u>-ee) **vi/vt**. *To worship*. Other uses of this highly versatile word include: 'to have a low opinion of one's self,' 'to be scared witless of the afterlife,' 'to believe in magic' and 'to be at a loose end on Sundays.' *(See also **Anoure**.)*

Hething. (<u>He</u>-thing) **n**. *Derision*. Along with a good deal of chinking *(see* **Chink**), hething is a universal response to the annual statement made by the government, on the day the school examinations results are released, that educational standards are higher today than ever before. Hething, however, turns rapidly to anger and incoherence when it is further claimed that such amazing advances have been made because today's pupils have been taught by those who are incomparably better than the dedicated, erudite, scholarly, grammatically accomplished and (whisper it softly) classically-educated schoolteachers one remembers from one's own schooldays.

Hight. (Hiyt) **vt**. *To embellish*. Or, as the word would be used by retired politicians about to publish their memoirs, 'to tell the plain, unvarnished truth.' *(See also* **Patefy**.*)*

Hilding. (<u>Hil</u>-ding) **n**. *A good-for-nothing*. As may be used to describe someone who, when offering to tarmac your drive, explains that he can give you a good price for the job because he's got a load of the stuff left over from another job. 'Tarmac,' incidentally, is derived from 'tærmakken,' an old Norse word meaning 'to spread a substance thinly by a process of scraping.'

Hippoid. (<u>Hip</u>-oyd) **n**. *A horse-like creature*. Often the sitter as well as the sat-upon.

Hirrient. (<u>Hi</u>-ree-'nt) **n**. *A snarling sound*. When a hirrient is elicited by the words 'Good dog,' it generally has the same effect as a starting pistol.

Hithe. (Hiydh) **n**. *A port*. In a storm, Fleetwood would serve – but it would have to be one hell of a storm.

Homiletical. (Ho-mi-<u>le</u>-ti-k'l, *or* Hoe-mi-<u>le</u>-ti-k'l) **a**. *Sociable*. In the Western Highlands of Scotland, this would refer to anyone who doesn't set the dogs on visitors.

Hoppestere. (<u>Hop</u>-e-steer) **n**. *A female dancer*.

> *In October 1958, Dame Felicia Strogova, prima ballerina with the Festival Ballet Company, was leaving the London Opera House after attending a performance of Benjamin Britten's opera* Peter Grimes, *when she trod on a broken gin bottle and cut her left foot badly. It seemed that she would not be able to dance in Henry Massingham's new production of* Giselle, *which was due to open in four weeks' time. When it was subsequently discovered that her understudy had fallen seriously ill, the whole future of the production was cast into doubt. It was the great choreographer Sir Charles Munt who saved the day by reworking Strogova's part of Giselle so that every dance could be performed using only one leg. Strogova hopped about the stage with such grace that she was the talk of London. However, Lynda Greebe, ballet critic of* The Times, *was incensed by what she regarded as Munt's unwarranted interference with the movements of classical ballet, and*

reviewed the production in scathing terms. Refusing to recognize Strogova as a ballerina, Greebe referred to her as 'no more than a hoppestere.' Strogova's heroic unipedal performance has, alas, long been forgotten, but Greebe's insult has entered the language as an alternative to 'ballerina.'

K. V. Houseman

Ballyhoo! Balletic Crises and Disasters (1998)

Horripilation. (Ho-ri-pi-<u>lae</u>-sh'n) **n**. *Creeping of the flesh*. The horripilation that occurs in response to terrifying visual or auditory stimuli is mild compared to that which can be elicited merely by thinking about those running the institutions to which we entrust our savings.

Hot cockles. (Hot-<u>ko</u>-k'lz) **n**. *A game in which one person covers his eyes and then has to guess which of several other players hits him*. An ancient game still highly popular in a number of Northumbrian villages where the inhabitants bear a close resemblance to each other, particularly in the closeness of the eyes and a certain lack of muscle tone around the mouth.

Howish. (<u>How</u>-ish) **a**. *Feeling vaguely indisposed*. Useful for describing the mild nausea brought on by reading one of Edwina Currie's novels. *(See also **Wamble**.)*

Hoyden. (<u>Hoy</u>-d'n) **n**. *An ill-bred woman*. Applicable in modern times to a career-oriented female who possesses all the qualities necessary for promotion to the highest editorial ranks of the popular press. *(See also **Callet**.)*

Huggery. (<u>Hu</u>-ger-ree) **n**. *The act of hugging.* A perfectly respectable activity, unless, that is, it's done to one behind one's back.

Humdudgeon. (Hum-<u>du</u>-j'n) **n**. *An imaginary illness.*

> *'A whining voice, a drooping stance –*
> *I diagnose humdudgeon,'*
> *The doctor said. 'And this the cure:*
> *The patient we must bludgeon.'*

Hydromancy. (<u>Hiy</u>-droe-man-see) **n**. *Divination by means of images seen in water.* There remain few practitioners of hydromancy, except in the Scottish highlands, where they enhance their divinatory powers by diluting the water with a single malt.

Hyle. (<u>Hiy</u>-lee) **n**. *The first matter to appear in the universe, and from which all else has been derived.* The origins of this word are obscure. It was Herbert Loomer, in *Where Words Come From* (1908), who put forward the currently accepted interpretation. Loomer recorded that in 1526 the Chinese astronomer Tao-Shi-Hon used the term 'hi-lee' to mean 'primal matter and those forces which operate upon it.' His choice of 'hi-lee' for this purpose is curious and has always puzzled etymologists because it was also the word used in his home province of Chian'zu to mean 'money.' Some clue to the mystery may, however, lie in Tao-Shi-Hon's statement that 'Hi-lee makes the world go round.'

Hypæthral. (Hiy-<u>pee</u>-thr'l) **a**. *Open to the sky*. A little-used word at the present time, but one which will probably prove useful to estate agents in Britain if global climate change produces the high winds that have been promised.

Hypotenuse. (Hiy-<u>po</u>-te-n*y*ooz) **n**. *That side of a right-angled triangle which subtends the right-angle*. A term used without any difficulty by past generations of British schoolchildren, but which nowadays has been consigned to the lexical dustbin. Regarded as a beastly foreign word which is far too difficult for modern children to pronounce, let alone understand, it has been replaced in modern maths courses by the eminently English, and readily pronounced, term 'the sloping side' ('sloping' as used to describe the forehead of whichever idiot thought this one up).

I

Icteritious. (Ik-ter-i̱-sh's) **a**. *Jaundiced*. Used of someone who's finally figured out how promotion works in British organizations, whatever their nature.

Ident. (I̱y-dent) **a**. *Hard-working*. A character defect which, if demonstrated to excess, inhibits essential activities such as attending committee meetings, and is therefore an absolute impediment to promotion prospects.

Idoneousness. (I̱y-<u>doe</u>-nee-us-n's) **n**. *Aptitude*. A factor which was once taken into account in the selection of students for university courses. Now that the majority of such courses do not require the students to show (or, indeed, ever to develop) an aptitude for anything, it has been safe to replace aptitude as a positive selection criterion with other factors, including: not being middle-class; being economically – and preferably also educationally – disadvantaged; being from an ethnic minority; and possessing as many physical disabilities as possible. *(See also **Docible** and **Indocibility**.)*

Ignicolist. (Ig-<u>ni</u>-ko-list) **n**. *One who worships fire.* An eminently suitable person to work in the basement of the Palace of Westminster. *(See also **Capnomancy**.)*

Illachrymable. (I-<u>lak</u>-ri-ma-b'l) **a**. *Incapable of being moved to tears.* A term used by Herbert Frothe MP, a former teacher of Greek and Latin at Malmesborough School, to describe members of the House of Commons Select Committee on Education, to whom he had just given evidence about the state of classical studies in British schools. Frothe later commented sadly that his remark had clearly been lost on the committee members, none of whom had received a classical education. *(See also **Larmoyant**.)*

Illation. (I-<u>lae</u>-sh'n) **n**. *An inference or deduction.* A conclusion which follows a careful, detailed and balanced consideration of all the evidence. The term is unlikely ever to be used by homœopaths.

Illeviable. (I-<u>le</u>-vee-a-b'l) **a**. *Unable to be levied.* Dr Friedrich Sigismund, in his bestselling *The Man Who Thought a Cat Was his Wife* (1995), which was based on his analysis of politicians' dreams, noted that 'illeviable' was the word used most frequently by three different Chancellors of the Exchequer when describing their worst nightmares.

Illigation. (I-li-<u>gae</u>-sh'n) **n**. *Entanglement.* A process refined and developed by bureaucrats in Brussels, and which is the only reason that most people can think of as to why Britain remains a member of the European Union.

Illth. (Ilth) **n**. *The opposite of wealth*. A leaked e-mail originating in the Department of Work and Pensions in 2006, and which was intended as a confidential briefing to the Prime Minister, contained the proposal to adopt 'illth' as a replacement for the term 'state pension.'

Imbonity. (Im-<u>bo</u>-ni-tee) **n**. *Unkindness*. A word that is inappropriately applied to the confinement of calves in veal crates, because it so breathtakingly understates the case. *(See also* **Immane**.*)*

Immane. (I-<u>maen</u>) **a**. *Inhumanly cruel or savage*. That's a better word for it. *(See* **Imbonity**, *above.)*

Immorigerousness. (I-mo-<u>ri</u>-jer-r's-n's) **n**. *Obstinate non-compliance*.

> *If all members of the teaching profession were to unite in immorigerousness towards all the paperwork imposed upon them as a result of one government educational 'initiative' after another, there would be nothing at all that the government could do about it. The only observable consequence would be a dramatic rise in educational standards.*
>
> J. Donald McFarlane
> *Education: A Revolution in Waiting* (2007)

Immund. (I-<u>mund</u>) **a**. *Foul*.

> *In 1998, the newly appointed Sudanese Foreign Minister, Ibrahim Wahziri El-Immund, who prided himself on his culinary skills, distributed a small, privately printed cookery book to his government colleagues. The book listed a hundred or so dishes of El-Immund's own devising, commencing with a recipe for Brussels sprout purée (cooking time three hours) and concluding with one for lamb kidney sorbet. Eight days after assuming office, El-Immund was assassinated by persons unknown, though it was widely believed at the time that the Prime Minister, whose wife had enthusiastically embraced El-Immund's culinary ethos, was implicated. Sir Godfrey Hadstock, whilst leading a trade mission to the Sudan, had been entertained by El-Immund during the latter's short period in office, and in later years always used the term 'immund' to mean any dish he found particularly repellent.*
>
> Wilhelmina Worthington
> *Culinary Calamities of the World* (2003)

Impone. (Im-<u>poen</u>) **vt**. *To wager*. As, for example, in imponing £50 that no-one can watch, without gagging, those television chefs who get their hands into any food they're preparing, periodically test how the cooking's going by licking a finger they've stuck into the stuff, and then arrange the meal on a plate without the assistance of anything resembling a spoon or fork. *(See also **Incocted**, **Keck** and **Omophagist**.)*

Impossibilist. (Im-p<u>o</u>-si-bi-list) **n**. *A proponent of a plan that cannot possibly work*. As, for example, Senator Selwyn D. Fosterbrook, who, on his appointment as United States peace envoy to the Middle East, claimed that he could establish an accord between Israel and the Palestinian Authority within a matter of days. 'It is,' he said, 'simply a question of persuading the two sides to be rational and tolerant, and for each of them to accept the other's right to freedom of religious expression.'

Impudicity. (Im-p*y*oo-<u>di</u>-si-tee) **n**. *Shamelessness*. That which permits a British or American politician to criticize electoral voting procedures in another country.

Incede. (In-<u>seed</u>) **vi**. *To move forward in a measured and unhurried manner*. A mode of progression adopted by every horse I've ever placed a bet on, apart from those that fell over.

Inclavate. (In-<u>kla</u>-vaet) **vt**. *To fix something firmly*. There is some variability in the meaning of this word, according to context. Thus, when used in the same sentence as the term 'flat-pack,' it means 'to achieve the impossible,' and when used in respect of the adjustable hinges on kitchen units, it means 'to strike ten or fifteen times with a hammer, whilst uttering high-pitched squealing noises, then call in the people who fitted the damned kitchen in the first place.'

Incocted. (In-<u>kok</u>-tid) **a**. *Uncooked*. And therefore probably safe to eat in a television chef's house. *(See also **Impone**, **Keck** and **Omophagist**.)*

Incruent. (<u>In</u>-kroo-'nt) **a**. *Without bloodshed*. As used, for example, to describe the civilized, democratic replacement of one politician by another following a free and fair election. It can also mean 'not completely satisfying.'

Indicium. (In-<u>di</u>-sh'm) **n**. *A sign*. Only the French could use road signs to raise issues of deep metaphysical significance, as, for example, by putting up one that says TOUTES DIRECTIONS right next to another that points the opposite way and says AUTRES DIRECTIONS.

Indite. (In-<u>diyt</u>) **vt**. *To put down in written form*. Though children nowadays refuse to believe it, there used to be lessons in primary schools on how to use a pen to produce legible words, correctly spelt and arranged neatly in a grammatically correct manner on a piece of paper. They also don't believe that the paper used had lines printed on it, and that it didn't have an inbuilt spell-check programme.

Indocibility. (In-doe-si-<u>bi</u>-li-tee) **n**. *The characteristic of being unteachable*. That which was regarded, long, long ago, as being an obstacle to going to university. *(See also **Docible** and **Idoneousness**.)*

Infandous. (In-<u>fan</u>-d's) **a**. *Unspeakable*. Finnish. *(See also* **Nefandous**.*)*

Infaust. (In-<u>forst</u>) **a**. *Unlucky*. Applicable to one whose house is not more than 30 metres above sea level if global warming turns out to be more than just a theory. *(See also* **Barr**.*)*

Injucundity. (In-ju-<u>kun</u>-di-tee) **n**. *Disagreeableness*. Part of the job description of anyone working in a London Underground ticket office.

Inscient. (<u>In</u>-sh'nt) **a**. *Lacking knowledge*. Once the decision had been made in British schools to replace the imparting of information with the need to 'engage with' the pupils, a lack of knowledge could no longer be any bar to achievement. Therefore, provided only that an inscient pupil is able to grasp a pencil in his clenched fist and make a mark with it, smooth and uninterrupted progression to a first-class degree at university is virtually assured.

Inspissate. (<u>In</u>-spi-saet) **a**. *To become thick or dense*. Used specifically of someone who has drunk eight or so pints of beer.

Insulse. (In-<u>suls</u>) **a**. *Tasteless*. As whoever advises Queen Elizabeth II on what to wear in public (particularly on her head).

Interamnian. (In-ter-<u>am</u>-nee-'n) **a**. *Between two rivers*. In the UK, low-lying interamnian sites are recognized by planning authorities as ideal for extensive new housing developments, particularly for people who like water features, preferably in their living rooms.

Inthronizate. (In-<u>throe</u>-ni-zaet) **vt**. *To enthrone*. A term that would undoubtedly be revived were an American to be made king.

Intumulate. (In-<u>tyoo</u>-myoo-laet) **vt**. *To bury*. What the Downing Street press office does to kill bad news, thereby providing, time after time, incontrovertible proof that reincarnation is not only possible but inevitable.

Inusitation. (In-*y*oo-si-<u>tae</u>-sh'n) **n**. *Disuse*. What plain English has fallen into amongst local government officials (civic administration facilitators).

Iotacism. (Iy-<u>oe</u>-ta-si-z'm) **n**. *Excessive use of 'I.'* The abuse of self-reference – a habit which, unless checked, leads to blindness to the needs of others.

Ipseity. (Ip-<u>see</u>-it-ee) **n**. *Personal identity*. Despite this metaphysical concept having received extensive attention from philosophers, particularly in regard to the relationship between 'I as known to myself,' 'I as known to others' and 'I as known only to God,' its precise meaning remains unresolved (except by financial institutions, who define it unequivocally as the state of possessing a recent gas bill).

Irenical. (Iy-<u>re</u>-ni-k'l) **a**. *Tending to resolve theological differences.* In the Middle East, an irenical vehicle may be either a written conciliatory communication between religious leaders or a car stuffed with home-made explosives.

Irpe. (Erp) **n**. *A toss of the head.* A French aristocrat's final gesture of defiance.

Irremeable. (I-<u>ree</u>-mee-a-b'l) **a**. *Permitting no return.* A term imported relatively recently from the French language. President Pompidou, on learning that thousands of British holidaymakers had been stranded in France as a result of yet another strike by French air traffic controllers, is reported to have said, '*Zut alors! C'est irréméable.*'

Isocracy. (Iy-<u>so</u>-kra-see) **n**. *A system of government in which political power is shared equally between all citizens.* This is, of course, the only true and workable form of democracy. When elected representation is introduced, democracy is inevitably replaced by ineptitocracy or fraudulentocracy, and usually by a mixture of both.

Ithyphallic. (I-thee-<u>fa</u>-lik) **a**. *Grossly indecent.* A term that is appropriately applied to the morally bankrupt policies of any government which happily expends millions of pounds on building up an arsenal of nuclear weapons, together with the means by which they may be 'delivered' (dropped on somebody), whilst at the same time failing to provide its citizens with clean drinking water and workable sewage systems, leaving such minor matters to be funded by charitable institutions such as Water Aid. *(See also **Largition**.)*

I-wald. (I-<u>wold</u>) **n**. *Power.*

> *The land he owned was bare and bleak –*
> *A high and windswept moor;*
> *His farmhouse tumbledown and cold,*
> *His wife and children poor.*
> *His sheep that huddled on the crags*
> *Were thin and bore few young;*
> *And from the meagre stony ground*
> *No sustenance was wrung.*
> *A letter from the government*
> *His fortune then restored.*
> *Its sentences were subtly phrased,*
> *And over it he pored.*
> *'The EU gives big grants,' it said,*
> *'And bank accounts it fills*
> *Of those who'll stick great turbines up*
> *And desecrate their hills.'*
> *The farmer's now a wealthy man;*
> *His palm's been crossed with gold.*
> *Huge whirring blades chop up the birds,*
> *And churn out wind i-wald.*

J

Jack-a-Lent. (Ja-ka-lent) **n**. *A person of no significance*. A term synonymous with 'voter,' as the latter is used inside the Palace of Westminster.

Jackeen. (Ja-<u>keen</u>) **n**. *A worthless but self-assertive individual*. A term synonymous with 'Member of Parliament,' as the latter is used outside the Palace of Westminster.

Jactation. (Jak-<u>tae</u>-sh'n) **n**. *An ostentatious display*. Used when talking about the ritualized courtship behaviour of ducks, or about soccer players who have just scored a goal.

Jargogle. (<u>Jar</u>-goe-g'l) **vt**. *To jumble*. Jargogling allows disparate things to come together by chance and in a manner that might not otherwise happen, sometimes with serendipitous consequences – which is probably why no great new idea ever came out of a tidy office.

Jauk. (Jork) **vi**. *To dawdle*. The means by which a child adjusts its mother's blood pressure.

Jesuitry. (<u>Je</u>-zwi-tree) **n**. *The achievement of a desired end by devious means.*

> 12. *When God had finished making the Earth, Satan, who was about to be expelled from Heaven, said to him: Before I am cast out of Heaven, I claim one thing: give me as my home the Earth that you have created.*
>
> 13. *God, however, would not accede to his wish, saying: That I cannot do, for the Earth is to become the home of men and women.*
>
> 14. *Satan was aggrieved, for he coveted the Earth, and was resentful that God should give it to the men and women of his creation. But Satan hid his anger, for he was cunning.*
>
> 15. *Then Satan said: I shall bow to your will, Lord, and make no claim to the Earth. Let it be that the Earth becomes the province of men and women.*
>
> 16. *And so it was. God created men and women to populate the Earth, where they prospered and multiplied. And Satan was patient. And the years and the generations passed.*
>
> 17. *And thus, in the fullness of time, it came about that Satan received, from those whom God had made, that which God had refused to give.*
>
> *Book of Jedeziah* (iii. 12–17)

Jillet. (<u>Ji</u>-l't) **n**. *A dizzy young woman.* The social consequences of mistaking a jillet for a flirtigig *(q.v.)* could be disastrous if the cause of her dizziness turns out to be an ear infection.

K

Kakistocracy. (Ka-ki-<u>sto</u>-kra-see) **n**. *A system of government in which the worst citizens hold the power.* The inevitable and entirely predictable consequence of electing those who wish to govern. *(See also* **Isocracy**.*)*

Keck. (Kek) **vi**. *To make a sound as though about to vomit.* As occurs in the phrase 'TV (keck, keck) chef.' *(See also* **Impone**, **Incocted** *and* **Omophagist**.*)*

Keek. (Keek) **vi**. *To peep.* The manner of looking that is associated with the greatest pleasure. The word derives from a salacious, privately printed book which circulated amongst the more degenerate sections of the aristocracy in or around 1780. Entitled *Samuel Keek's Diary*, the book described in detail a number of boudoir scenes as observed through the keyhole.

Kef. (Kef) **n**. *The derivation of pleasure from idleness.* May also now be used to mean 'the appreciation of conceptual art.'

Ket. (Ket) **n**. *Raw flesh.*

> *In France, any meat is regarded as raw that has been kept below*
> *room temperature; exposure of meat to room temperature leads*
> *to its being classed as cooked, whilst exposing it to anything*
> *above room temperature results in its being sent away from the*
> *table as overcooked. In Montreal, Canada, the phrase* 'être
> viandé' *means 'to die in France.'*

Giles Maudsley

Continental Digestive Ailments (1994)

Kibble. (<u>Ki</u>-b'l) **vi**. *To grind coarsely.*

> *As sweet Salome shed her veils,*
> *And showed how she could kibble,*
> *King Herod, though as hard as nails,*
> *Began to sweat and dribble.*

Killcrop. (<u>Kil</u>-krop) **n**. *A brat.* A child whose concerns centre purely upon self-gratification, and whose future thus lies either in politics or in prison; if in the first, then deservedly also in the second.

Kim-kam. (<u>Kim</u>-kam) **a**. *Crooked.* A word of relatively recent origin, having been first used, and apparently invented, by US General Miles K. Newhaven in his memoirs (*Talking to the Enemy*, 2007); General Newhaven derived the term from the name of Kim Kam Lo, the North Korean chief negotiator at the 2005 talks on nuclear non-proliferation.

Kinchin-lay. (<u>Kin</u>-chin-lae) **n**. *Theft of money from a child who has been sent out on an errand*. The founding principle of commerce.

Kithe. (Kiydh) **vt**. *To make something known*. Research into the use of information technology in education has demonstrated that a computer can now kithe partially in three hours what would once have taken a teacher with a stick of chalk as long as three minutes to kithe in full.

Knipperdolling. (<u>Ni</u>-per-do-ling) **n**. *A religious fanatic*. Someone whom it would be useful, satisfying, and probably very easy, to persuade that the surest way of getting into Paradise is by drinking bleach.

L

Lab. (Lab) **n**. *A tell-tale*. At one time, such creatures, when found at school, were treated with contempt and thence-forth shunned, but (so far has the country gone to the dogs) they are now regarded as model pupils.

Labefaction. (La-bi-<u>fak</u>-sh'n) **n**. *Downfall*. A term most appropriately used when the downfall is caused by the beastly work of a lab *(q.v.)*.

Lackland. (<u>Lak</u>-land) **n**. *A person who possesses no land*. It would be entirely appropriate to use this as a synonym of 'mankind,' because land is never possessed – though one may, for a brief time, have the use of it. The failure to grasp this simple concept has resulted in almost as many wars as have been caused by religion.

Ladify. (<u>Lae</u>-dee-fiy) **vt**. *To make a lady of someone*. An end usually achieved only over a long period – sometimes many years – by careful and extended tuition in deportment, elocution, choice of appropriate attire, and the close observance of the rules of social etiquette. In Casablanca, however, the effect is attained within a matter of minutes by cutting things short.

Ladrone. (La-<u>droen</u>) **n**. *A highwayman*. At one time, this word was applied only to a person who illegally extorted money from the occupants of carriages. The replacement of carriages by motor cars has been followed by the legalization of this activity, the ladrone now appearing in a number of guises. *(See also* **Grassant**.*)*

Læotropic. (Lee-oe-<u>troe</u>-pik) **a**. *Having a tendency to turn to the left*.

> *His policies are socialist –*
> *Financially myopic.*
> *Some think that he is sinister*
> *For being læotropic.*

Laidly. (<u>Laed</u>-lee) **a**. *Hideous*. When used at a fashion show in Milan, Paris or London, the term can take on the meaning of 'fabulous.'

Laigh. (Laekh) **n**. *A low point*. That which occurs just as you are sitting down to dinner and your host tells you that the wine you'll be drinking is 'a lovely fruity red we brought back from our holiday in Romania.'

Lambency. (<u>Lam</u>-ben-see) **n**. *A brilliant display of wit*. A term which also embodies the concept of 'latency,' and so may be used to refer to the razor-sharp verbal riposte that occurs to one several hours after it would have been useful.

Lamia. (<u>Lae</u>-mee-a) **n**. *A ferocious mythical beast with the body of a woman and a taste for human flesh.*

> *Those Cabinet members of the Thatcher government who had received a classical education (almost all of them) used to refer to the Prime Minister, in her absence, as 'Lamia.' When, on one occasion, she arrived in the Cabinet Room unannounced and overheard the soubriquet being used, she enquired as to the subject of the conversation. The Cabinet Secretary, Sir Elwin Manning, narrowly averted disaster by explaining that the discussion was of a pantomime currently showing at the Dulwich Hippodrome, which featured a comic character called Lamia Negge.*
>
> Niall Greenbank CBE
> *Memoirs of a Civil Servant* (1990)

Land-damn. (<u>Land</u>-dam) **vt**. *To contrive a hell on earth for some-one*. A word that could usefully be used in the sense of 'to design a traffic-calming system.'

Laniate. (<u>La</u>-nee-aet) **vt**. *To shred*. Or, in the case of those useful information newsletters mailed at considerable public expense by the local authority to all householders, the term can also mean 'to file carefully, for future reference.' *(See also **Gliff**.)*

Largition. (Lar-ji-sh'n) **n**. *The act of giving bountifully.* What one may engage in with no more than a button or two and a few metal washers if the charity envelope has an adhesive flap. This may be done with an entirely clear conscience if the charitable donation is destined for a country possessing nuclear weapons. *(See also **Ithyphallic**.)*

Larmoyant. (Lar-moy-'nt) **a**. *Tearful.* As used by international observers at the funeral of the Beloved Supreme Leader of North Korea, to describe the people's outward expression of their inner indifference. *(See also **Illachrymable**.)*

Larrup. (La-r'p) **vt**. *To thrash.* That which, at one time, was done to a lab *(q.v.)* or a custron *(q.v.)*, instead of, as now, making them European Commissioners.

Lask. (Lask) **vi**. *To suffer looseness of the bowels.* What happens to you if you open your front door and find Germaine Greer on the doorstep.

Latescent. (Lae-te-s'nt) **a**. *Becoming hidden.* What any right-minded person would think of doing on spotting Germaine Greer coming up the front path. *(See **Lask**.)*

Latibulize. (La-<u>ti</u>-byoo-liyz) **vi**. *To get into a hiding place.* Whilst shouting to those you hold dear, 'Quick! She's coming.' *(See Latescent.)*

Latitancy. (<u>La</u>-ti-tan-see, *or sometimes* <u>Lae</u>-ti-tan-see) **n**. *The state of remaining hidden.* Which usually comes to an end only following an affirmative answer to the question 'Has that cruentous *(q.v.)* woman gone yet?' *(See **Latibulize**.)*

Latrant. (<u>Lae</u>-trant) **a**. *Barking.*

> *After unveiling the plaque and declaring the new Outpatient Department open, the Prince spoke for thirty-five minutes about the need for complementary therapies to be widely available as part of the NHS. He ended by commending to the medical staff the work of Saanjeeva Vilinathan in northern India on the use of cosmic life-energy emitted by powdered bamboo to treat migraine and broken legs.*

> [Applause. Ten-year-old Abigail-Mary Bertwistle, daughter of the hospital Bed Manager, presented the Prince with an eight-pound blue crystal mounted on a silver plinth.]

> *Consultant neurosurgeon Mr Cardew Sprigg-Frodde then rose to thank the Prince for visiting the hospital and for giving the medical staff a rare opportunity to listen to someone so clearly latrant.*

> Minutes of the Management Committee,
Carthorpe Hospital (15 August 1989)

Latrede. (La-<u>treed</u>) **a**. *Slow*. That aspect of the psychological make-up of distinguished visitors to Carthorpe Hospital that has been responsible, on a number of occasions, for saving Mr Cardew Sprigg-Frodde's medical career. *(See **Latrant**.)*

Latrociny. (La-<u>troe</u>-si-nee) **n**. *Brigandage*. Following a particularly productive raid, it was the practice of the leader of the brigands to keep for himself the largest portion of the spoils, sharing the rest out between the members of his gang in accordance with the degree of effort that they had put into the theft. The term may be appropriately applied in modern times to the system under which large bonuses are awarded to those working (a term which one uses loosely) in the financial services industry. *(See also **Facient**.)*

Lautitious. (Lor-<u>ti</u>-sh's) **a**. *Sumptuous*. In Doncaster, this describes a meal where butter is spread on the bread before the jam is applied.

Laxist. (<u>Lak</u>-sist) **n**. *A person who favours loose interpretations of the evidence*. In the USA, where this word is synonymous with 'creationist,' it is sometimes deliberately misspelt as 'laskist' *(see **Lask**)*, to indicate the effect that any such individuals who aspire to (and often attain) high political office have upon those who know which end of a fork to hold.

Leal. (Leel) **a**. *Genuine*. A term which could be useful in the fashion industry to refer to any garment that is recognizable as a 'designer' item by its distinctive label. Other meanings include: (1) made in Malaysia; (2) available on the internet for £2; and (3) hanging on a rail outside a shop in Morecambe.

Leam. (Leem) **n**. *A gleam of light*. Used metaphorically of a hint that a currently dire state of affairs is to be transformed infinitely for the better; as, for example, a rumour that the Director General of the BBC is to be replaced by a halibut. *(See also **Flump** and **Fnese**.)*

Lear. (Leer) **n**. *Learning*. What, years ago, the working classes acquired in order to better themselves, but what those of their grandchildren who are now in government regard as something which, like being working class (or, indeed, working), is to be looked down upon.

Lecanomancy. (<u>Le</u>-ka-noe-man-see) **n**. *Telling the future by gazing into water*. A skill that used to come naturally to normal, healthy boys who had successfully acquired the patina that only grubbing around under bushes and foraying into dark and dusty garden sheds can produce; faced with water, they could divine like a shot that the immediate future would be wet, soapy, and almost unimaginably horrid. The skill has, however, largely been lost in the face of health-and-safety regulations which forbid children to be released within a hundred yards of a bush, and by the replacement of the garden shed by the computer as a source of childish delight. *(See also **Hydromancy**.)*

Lede. (Leed) **n**. *A nation.* What Scotland will be if the Scottish Nationalists have their way, and what England will never be if they don't.

Leden. (Lay-den) **n**. *A nation's language.* That which in Britain used to be the primary medium for the expression of our highest cultural achievements and aspirations, permitting us to demonstrate by how far we had transcended our animal origins. Now that is has been decided by educationalists that our language has nothing to do with grammar, punctuation, spelling, pronunciation, or an understanding of the origins of words, it functions only as the means by which people express their desires, thereby revealing just how short the evolutionary road has actually been. *(See also **Streel**.)*

Leeful. (Lee-ful) **a**. *Just.*

> *When Alice Burns was woken*
> *By noises in the night,*
> *She neither rose in panic,*
> *Nor felt a moment's fright.*
>
> *For Alice Burns was ready*
> *To have a little fun.*
> *Beneath her little pillow*
> *She kept a little gun.*
>
> *The bedroom door was opened,*
> *And in the burglar crept.*
> *He rummaged through the casket*
> *Where necklaces were kept.*

Then Alice switched the light on.
'You won't find jewels there,'
She told the burglar, smiling.
'I'm not a millionaire!'

The burglar turned in horror:
This wasn't what he'd planned!
'Hello,' said Alice, coolly,
And shot him through the hand.

'All right,' the burglar shouted,
'Don't shoot, and then I'll go.'
But Alice aimed her firearm
And shot him through the toe.

'You'll pay for that,' he bellowed.
'I'll really make you beg!'
But Alice pulled the trigger
And shot him through the leg.

The burglar now was livid,
And lunged towards the bed.
'Goodbye,' said Alice sweetly
And shot him through the head.

The Judge was old and crusty;
He said, 'You'll go to jail.
For what you did was deadly —
And quite beyond the pale.'

> *But Alice had a lawyer*
> *Who got her off the hook.*
> *He used a legal loophole*
> *Found in a dusty book.*
>
> *It said, 'When masked intruders*
> *Are shot, and bite the dust,*
> *Some think that that's illegal.*
> *It is — but only Just.'*

Leguleian. (Le-gyoo-<u>lee</u>-an) **a**. *Pettifogging*. The term derives from the name of Leguleia, Queen of Dysos, who decreed a number of totally pointless laws. One, for example, required all unmarried men to carry a peacock feather in public, whilst another forbade the use of the colour green in any garment worn above the waist. Leguleia took the view that if the people could be persuaded to conform to such pettifogging laws, they would even more readily obey the laws that were truly important.

Lek. (Lek) **n**. *A congregation*. The bored addressed by the boring (and vice versa).

Lenitude. (<u>Le</u>-ni-tyood) **n**. *Smoothness*.

> *There's nothing like plenitude*
> *For engendering lenitude —*
> *The behavioural oil*
> *That makes one recoil.*

Lenocinant. (Len-<u>oe</u>-si-n'nt) **a**. *Tending to incite to evil deeds.* Those who have reason to do so can readily provide abundant evidence that this is an attribute of any holy text you care to mention.

Lepadoid. (<u>Le</u>-pa-doyd) **a**. *Barnacle-like.* Useful for describing a cabinet minister's attachment to his job in the face of overwhelming evidence of a staggering degree of incompetence or of a level of criminality that would put an ordinary citizen behind bars for years. *(See also **Muculent**.)*

Lepidity. (Le-<u>pi</u>-di-tee) **n**. *Facetiousness.* A degree of irresponsible levity that would never be seen in a lexicographer.

Lethe. (<u>Lee</u>-thee) **n**. *The waters of oblivion.*

> *The waters of oblivion,*
> *In Hades flowing deep,*
> *The curse of memory dispel,*
> *So that the dead may sleep.*

There are times (trying to buy screws of the right size and shape in a so-called DIY supermarket is just one of them) when a Lethe and tonic would go down nicely. *(But see also **Lew**.)*

Levigable. (<u>Le</u>-vi-ga-b'l) **a**. *Capable of being polished.* A box containing several hundred small shiny objects, all of which are levigable, makes a perfect gift on any occasion for someone with obsessive-compulsive disorder.

Lew. (Lyoo) **vt**. *To warm*. When it seems that a draught of Lethe *(q.v.)* would be just the thing, a decent bottle of claret lewed to just above room temperature makes a reasonable substitute – and avoids the inconvenience of having to pay a disagreeable old gentleman to ferry you across the Styx.

Limbeck. (<u>Lim</u>-bek) **vi**. *To make a strong mental effort to come up with ideas*. What a lexicographer has to do somewhere around the letter 'L.'

Lingism. (<u>Ling</u>-i-z'm) **n**. *The treatment of obesity using gymnastic exercises*. Based upon the work of the Swedish physician Dr Holger Ling (1897), after whom the system was named, this method of treating morbid obesity owes its modern form to Dr Angus Broom, whose book *Jump Off Your Fat* (1973) headed the nonfiction bestseller list in the UK for twenty-eight consecutive months. The theoretical justification for Lingism was based upon the principle of 'metabolic harmonization,' but Professor Helena Margolis, in 2004, showed conclusively that any weight reduction achieved as a result of engaging in Broom's programme of gymnastic exercises was due entirely to muscle fatigue, the patients being too weak to pick up a knife and fork.

Logocracy. (Lo-<u>go</u>-kra-see) **n**. *A system of government in which words rule*. This term encompasses all systems of government, though the ways in which words exert their controlling power differ from one system to another. Thus in a parliamentary democracy words operate by inducing feelings of weariness and resignation; in a technocracy they work through obfuscation and by engendering a sense of inferiority; in an autocracy the only two words needed are 'shut' and 'up.'

Logodædalus. (Lo-goe-<u>dee</u>-da-l's) **n**. *A person skilled in the art of persuasion by the use of words.* Dædalus, father of Icarus, was not only a skilled artisan but was also said to be an accomplished orator. His name, which became a synonym for 'a persuasive speaker,' was assigned in the mid-19th century as an accolade in a number of Oxford colleges to the student voted best debater of the year. In each of the years 1851, 1852 and 1853, Oriel College bestowed the title of Dædalus upon Thomas Halsey, who, being only four feet two inches tall, was obliged to deliver his speeches whilst standing upon a section of tree trunk that had been hewn for that purpose (and which Halsey took everywhere with him, dragging it behind him in a small wooden cart). A common sight in Oxford over the three years that Halsey was a student there, the tree trunk upon which he stood during debates became known as the 'Log of Dædalus,' later contracted to the 'Log o' Dædalus.' The title of Dædalus was abandoned in 1866, for reasons that remain obscure, but the term 'Log o' Dædalus,' further contracted to 'Logodædalus,' passed into general English usage to mean 'one who uses words in such a way that some people will believe anything.'

Loring. (<u>Lor</u>-ring) **n**. *Teaching*. Loring in today's schools consists in large measure of not interrupting the pupils when they are using their computers (or, of course, their mobile phones).

Lorn. (Lorn) **a**. *Doomed*.

> *'Cross dewy field, through shadowed dell,*
> *She treads the misty morn;*
> *Whilst shyly through the thinning clouds,*
> *Peeks out the face of dawn*
> *Upon the maid who weeps alone –*
> *By love and loving lorn.*

Loselry. (<u>Loe</u>-z'l-ree) **n**. *Profligacy*. A word originally introduced into the language by Professor Malachi J. Burton in his scholarly work *Economic Strategy: An Analysis* (1993). Burton took it from the name of his erstwhile Cambridge tutor, Heinz Friedrich Losel, an Austrian emigré who, in the early nineteen-fifties, following a series of what were subsequently diagnosed as small strokes, confused British pounds and Austrian groschen (the latter then being worth around one ten-thousandth of a pound), and became spectacularly bankrupt within the space of thirteen days after buying two Rolls-Royces, a Monet, three Fabergé eggs and most of the arable land in Cambridgeshire. Burton used the term to mean any policy upon which local government spending is based.

Lutarious. (Loo-<u>tair</u>-ee-'s) **a**. *Living in mud*. Research reported in the journal *Contemporary Molecular Genetics* showed a
98.6% overlap between the DNA of editors of tabloid newspapers and that of single-celled lutarious organisms.

Luxurist. (<u>Luks</u>-yur-rist) **n**. *Someone who revels in luxury*. In
Brixton, this is taken to mean anyone who has replaced the
plywood in their windows with glass.

M

Mabble. (<u>Ma</u>-b'l) **vt**. *To wrap up the head*. A common request in a French boucherie (*'Voulez-vous la mabbler, s'il vous plaît?'*).

Macrology. (Ma-<u>kro</u>-lo-jee) **n**. *The use of more words than desirable*. Dr Ernst Vogler demonstrated to the delegates attending the Annual Conference of Antimacrologists, held in Padua in 2006, that any of Jane Austen's novels could, without loss of plot or emotional content, be reduced to three pages, including the title page.

Maculose. (<u>Ma</u>-kyoo-loez) **a**. *Spotted*. According to the recently unearthed memoirs of Gloria Stopes-Brydle, a once prominent member of the Bloomsbury set, every dinner hosted by Virginia Woolf ended with a serving of 'maculose dick,' accompanied each time by the same joke, at which everyone felt obliged to laugh.

Madefy. (<u>Ma</u>-di-fiy) **vt**. *To make wet*. This would probably be most useful in modern usage in its very specific and British sense of 'to soften a person's moral fibre.' Examples of madefying would include persuading a fellow to play bridge, drink Campari-soda, watch synchronized swimming, or listen to Frank Sinatra.

Maffle. (<u>Ma</u>-f'l) **vi**. *To waste time*. As, for example, in giving the slightest thought to any subject on which the government calls for a 'public debate' before it drafts legislation on the matter. On certain days, 'maffle' can also mean 'to get out of bed.' *(See also **Afterpiece** and **Berattle**.)*

Magnale. (Mag-<u>nar</u>-lee) **n**. *A marvellous thing*. In an age when the great adventures (flying into space, conquering the world's highest mountains, walking to the poles, exploring the depths of the ocean) have all been filmed and documented, one must seek nature's magnales on a smaller scale. The thrill is, however, no less satisfying when one is discovered – as, for example, upon unexpectedly encountering someone who knows (or cares) that the 'o' in 'covert' is pronounced like that in 'covered.' If you don't believe it, check with the OED – or, even better, think about it.

Magsman. (<u>Magz</u>-m'n) **n**. *One who obtains money under false pretences*. As, for example, a bookseller who puts autobiographies on the nonfiction shelves.

Maieutical. (Miy-<u>yoo</u>-ti-k'l) **a**. *Describes a Socratic technique by means of which one person assists another in bringing to full intellectual fruition thoughts and ideas that would otherwise have remained hidden*. It is a tribute to the spirit of tolerance that characterizes the British government that this country maintains any diplomatic and trade links with a dozen or more states in which the maieutical element is introduced into discussions with their citizens less by the sensitive application of Socratic procedures than by the application of electrodes to sensitive parts of the body. *(See also* **Ultroneous.***)*

Mainour. (<u>Mae</u>-n'r) **n**. *A stolen item found in the thief's possession.* The primary contemporary use of this word is in the legal phrase 'to be discovered with the mainour,' though in 1983 it was used in a speech by Sir Eric Fairfax, Deputy Director of the National Institute of Fiscal Research, when referring to 'the entire contents of Her Majesty's Treasury.' Though meant jocularly, the term stuck for a while, and it was even suggested that the 'Treasury' be renamed the 'Stash.'

Malapert. (<u>Ma</u>-la-pert) **a**. *Impudent.* A quality that at one time would have met with instant and clear disapproval, but which we are now increasingly required to accept as a necessary condition of modern life. Thus, a malapert attitude is displayed by GPs' receptionists (now referred to as 'trained medical advisers') who ask, in the full hearing of everyone in the waiting room, why you want to see the doctor (to which, incidentally, the most effective response is to lean forward until you are as close as possible to the questioner's face and say, in a confidental whisper, 'I have a sexually transmitted disease of the mouth.')

Malengin. (Ma-<u>len</u>-jin) **n**. *Evil intent*. The only conceivable reason for cooking tripe.

Mammothrept. (<u>Ma</u>-moe-thrept) **n**. *A spoilt child*. Also useful in referring to a sportsman who, irrespective of whether his team has won or lost, does not take the first opportunity to congratulate the members of the other side. Some people find it interesting, when watching televised football matches, to count the number of players who may, at the end of each game, be described as mammothrepts. *(See also* **Glump**.*)*

Manavilins. (Ma-<u>na</u>-vi-linz) **n**. *Odds and ends*. An ideal use for this term would be as a collective noun for those objects which possess no conceivable use or importance until they are thrown away – at which point they become crucial components of the most highly complex and expensive equipment in the house, on which the warranty has just expired.

Mangonist. (<u>Man</u>-go-nist) **n**. *A seller of goods of low quality*. Named after Alphonsine Mangon, a French seamstress who from 1867 to 1898 supplied clothes to most of the well-to-do ladies in Paris. In October 1898, Madame Mangon was arrested when it was discovered that the material of the garments she sold, though possessing the appearance of fine silk, was actually made from waste paper by a process invented by her brother, Alphonse. This came to light only when the Vicomtesse de Maury was caught in an exceptionally heavy rainstorm, and her dress (and, according to the gossip of the day, a good part of her underwear) turned into a kind of porridge. However, all charges against Madame Mangon were subsequently dismissed when it became apparent that no lady who had been duped into purchasing clothes from her would admit it, and thus all testimony against her collapsed.

Marrer. (<u>Mar</u>-rer) **n**. *One who destroys*. In America, this has also been used to mean 'one who liberates others from an oppressive regime.' Whilst the premise that destruction is a necessary prelude to reconstruction is at least debatable, the assumption that reconstruction is an inevitable consequence of destruction is demonstrably false.

Meed. (Meed) **vt**. *To bribe*. To engage in the process by which the Saudi royal family may be reassured as to the quality of British fighter planes.

Menticulture. (<u>Men</u>-ti-kul-ch'r) **n**. *Cultivation of the mind*. In Britain this was once regarded as one of the two guiding principles of education, the other being to provide pupils with the factual information and conceptual knowledge needed to exercise their developing mental faculties. These principles have now been set aside in favour of a more literal interpretation of 'cultivation,' which involves the provision of a liberal supply of manure.

Messan. (<u>Me</u>-san) **n**. *A lapdog*. Being a mere degenerative descendant of noble ancestral stock, and no longer capable of independent existence, the messan is dominated by the whims and caprices of its owner. Curiously, the term was recently also used to mean 'a recipient of the US Congressional Medal of Honor.'

Methodology. (Me-th'-<u>do</u>-lo-jee) **n**. *The science or study of method (more accurately, discourse about method).* Although this word has not been lost, its meaning has. It is now incorrectly used instead of 'method' by those who wish, but fail, to appear educated. The modern affliction of inappropriate word expansion extends well beyond the method–methodology confusion, occurring with increasing frequency elsewhere in the language, as, for example, in the use of 'simplistic' to mean 'simple,' 'opportunistic' to mean 'opportune' and 'fortuitous' to mean 'fortunate.'

Metromania. (Me-troe-<u>mae</u>-nee-a) **n**. *A compulsion to write verses.* The term was introduced into medical terminology in 1982 by Dr Henri Foucault, a psychiatrist at the Hôpital Sainte-Claire, Paris. Foucault described the case of a mentally disturbed young woman, one of whose more florid symptoms was an overwhelming desire to write poetry of appalling sentimentality whilst travelling between Étoile and Opéra.

Minauderie. (Min-<u>or</u>-dree) **n**. *Coquetry.* The form that this takes varies greatly from region to region within the UK. Thus, in Bristol it involves a slight turning away of the head whilst simultaneously giving a lingering sideways glance; in

Preston it is achieved by grinning broadly (but seductively) with a mouth full of chips.

Misdo. (Mis-<u>doo</u>) **vt**. *To do evil*. To do that which lives after one, the rest being interred with one's bones. Can also mean 'to be a script writer for *The Archers*.' *(See also* **Wite**.*)*

Misgo. (Mis-<u>goe</u>) **vi**. *To go astray*. In most English boys' grammar schools in the 1950s, this term meant specifically 'to play – or even to watch – rugby league.' Showing as much as even a passing interest in soccer was regarded as being so far beyond misgoing as to present clear evidence of moral degeneracy.

Misprisal. (Mis-<u>priy</u>-z'l) **n**. *Disdain*. There could be no greater expression of misprisal than that which was, in the good old days, shown towards those who succumbed to the urge to misgo *(q.v.)*. *O, sic transit gloria scholae.*

Mobile. (<u>Moe</u>-bi-lee, *not* <u>Moe</u>-bi-lae *– it's not necessary to show that you know that it's Latin*) **n**. *The rabble*. Especially useful for referring to those in the theatre who haven't switched off their telephones.

Mome. (Moem) **n**. *A fool*. Also used adjectivally to describe a rath that outgrabes.

Monocephalous. (Mon-oe-<u>ke</u>-fa-l's) **a**. *Possessing only one head*. But remarkably, in politicians, two faces.

Mop. (Mop) **vi**. *To grimace*. As upon discovering the price of a cup of tea in a motorway service station, but more particularly upon tasting the stuff after having bought it.

Morbific. (Mor-<u>bi</u>-fik) **a**. *Disease-causing*. Although once employed to refer specifically to pathogenic organisms, this useful term may now be appropriately applied to hospitals, cruise liners, and countries where the meat on your plate may once have been able to bark.

Morigeration. (Mo-ri-jer-<u>rae</u>-sh'n) **n**. *Obedience*.

> *Obedience is an expression of an essentially unstable state in which one party stands in subordinate relationship to another. Cooperation, however, represents a stable consensual relationship between two parties, neither of whom assumes dominance over the other. Noncooperation leads to the breakdown of an ordered society; disobedience is the means by which a repressive regime is overthrown. The course of human history is determined by the extent to which the people come to recognize and to understand the difference between obedience and cooperation, and the strength of their desire to replace the one by the other.*

> Günter Weiss, translated by Juliet Kees
> *The Forces That Shape the World* (1954)

Morne. (Morn) **a**. *Dismal*. As used to describe the performance of any comedy duo since the demise of Morecambe and Wise.

Morology. (Mo-<u>rol</u>-o-jee) **n**. *Fools' talk*. Suitably qualified reflexologists, aromatherapists, crystal healers, and practitioners of a wide range of other complementary therapies, will soon be able to enrol with the University of Congleton to study for a Bachelor of Science degree in Morology.

Mournival. (<u>Moor</u>-ni-v'l) **n**. *A foursome of anything*. The word was first used by Sarah Jane Loop in her novel *Taking It With You* (1977), in which the hero, funeral director Titus Ulvers, comments that:

> 'A Carnival, to be a success, requires the attendance of a multitude. Only four, however, are needed for the perfect burial – a grave-digger, a priest, one mourner and, of course, a corpse – what you might call a Mournival, I suppose.'

Though Miss Loop's novel was not a resounding literary success (the print-run was pulped after no more than sixteen copies were sold in the course of three years, two copies being publicly burnt in Norwich), the term 'mournival' was briefly seized upon as a valuable contribution to English vocabulary, and by the end of the seventies could be heard in virtually every conversation. Its meaning eventually became generalized to any group of four people, as in the popular saying 'One's alone; two's company, three's a crowd and four's a mournival.' The demise of the word may be traced precisely to 20 August 1983 after the literary critic of *The Times*, Aloysius Monk, condemned it as 'a typical creation of Loop – quintessentially Loopy.'

Mouth-glue. (<u>Mowth</u>-gloo) **n**. *Any glue activated by moistening with the tongue*. Also, in an ideal world, a drink served in the House of Commons.

Muckibus. (<u>Mu</u>-ki-bus) **a**. *Drunk*. Useful when referring to Everton supporters returning home after an away match, and could also be used substantively to mean the coach in which they are travelling.

Muculent. (<u>Myoo</u>-kyoo-l'nt) **a**. *Slimy*. A politician who offers 'an administrative oversight' as an explanation for financial irregularities is aptly described as muculent, and is almost certainly lepadoid *(q.v.)* too.

Muliebrity. (M<u>y</u>oo-lee-<u>e</u>-bri-tee) **n**. *Womanliness*. Also, curiously, stubbornness.

Mullock. (<u>Mu</u>-l'k) **n**. *Rubbish*.

> *'Mullock' is a word invented quite accidentally in 2004 by John Fergus McCreadie, a teacher in a small primary school near Inverbreechie, Aberdeenshire. McCreadie asked an eight-year-old pupil, Jamie Intyre, to name the tip of the long Scottish promontory to the west of the Isle of Arran. When Jamie said 'Islay', McCreadie replied, 'No — that's Mull o' Kintyre.' What wee Jamie heard, however, was 'No! That's Mullock, Intyre.' Assuming that 'mullock' must mean (at the very least) 'rubbish,' Jamie that evening tearfully recounted the incident to his parents, and they, also not having heard the word 'mullock'*

before, accepted their son's interpretation. McCreadie was suspended, and later dismissed, by the education authorities for verbally abusing a pupil. 'Mullock' became assimilated into the language following extensive news media coverage of McCreadie's unsuccessful appeal against his dismissal. Costs were awarded against McCreadie, who was bankrupted as a consequence.

J. Fergus MacFrisbie
Speaking of the Highlands (2006)

(See also **Cultch** *and* **Peltry***.)*

Mumpsimus. (<u>Mump</u>-si-m's) **n**. *An opponent of change.* Also, a person of experience.

Mussitate. (<u>Mu</u>-si-taet) **vi/vt**. *To mutter.*

The word has its origins in an amalgam of 'Mussolini' and 'hesitate,' and was originally used to describe the indecisiveness of those who led the anti-Fascist movement in pre-war Italy. Unable to reach agreement on how best to rid the country of Mussolini, they were reduced to grumbling, or 'mussitating,' about his inexorable rise to power.

G. L. Harrison (Editor)
Words Weird and Wonderful (2006)

Mutuate. (<u>Myoo</u>-tyoo-aet) **vt**. *To borrow.* Or, when books or garden tools are involved, 'to keep.'

Mysterize. (<u>Mi</u>-ster-riyz) **vi / vt**. *To adopt a mystical interpretation.* The way in which those of little learning and less sense seek to understand the world.

Mythometer. (Mith-<u>o</u>-mi-t'r) **n**. *A means of assessing the power of a myth.* In 1936, the *Journal of Mythological Studies* carried an article describing Charles Thornton-Birt's 'scale of mythological power,' which ranged from 0 (a myth believed by no-one) to 10 (one that was believed by everyone). Ratings were determined by first reading a myth to a large number of adults and then determining the percentage of people who thought it believable. Thornton-Birt wrote a number of influential books based upon his assessments of myths. In his later years, however, he became disillusioned with the usefulness of his technique when he found that 997 out of a group of 1000 people who had voted for George W. Bush's second term believed every single myth presented to them, including the one describing the way the world had been constructed out of old tractor tyres by three golden pigs.

N

Nagualism. (N'-<u>gwar</u>-li-z'm) **n**. *The name given to a now-defunct South American system of superstitious ideas and beliefs.* A word which may usefully be revived as a collective noun for those 'therapeutic' procedures describing themselves as 'alternative,' or 'complementary,' particularly if they employ explanatory concepts involving terms such as 'lines of force,' or anything at all to do with 'energy.'

Nayward. (<u>Nae</u>-w'd) **n** *and* **a**. *The negative side; hence 'to the nayward' comes to signifiy 'towards unbelief.'*

RIP
JOHN FRANCIS PARTRIDGE
CURATE OF THIS PARISH
(1813–1887)
'TWAS DOUBT THAT MADE HIM WAYWARD,
'TWAS SHE THAT SAVED HIM THEN —
BUT DROVE HIM TO THE NAYWARD
BY KISSING OTHER MEN.

Nefandous. (Ne-<u>fan</u>-d's) **a**. *Unspeakable*. In 1927, the anthropologist Hermione Ingle, whose impartiality as an observer of other cultures was compromised by her intense dislike of anyone who was not English, published her magnum opus, *Trapoa: An Anthropological Analysis*. This described the daily life and customs of the Trapoan islanders, whose religion decreed that they should wash their bodies only once every six months, and whose language consisted almost exclusively of hisses and glottal stops. Ingle, who spent what she spoke of as 'easily the three worst years of my life' with the islanders, without ever achieving the slightest success in communicating with them, memorably referred in her book to 'the nefandous language of a nefandous people.' When she died, in 1965, she left £30,000 in her will to fund a prize (as yet unclaimed) for the first person to introduce the Trapoans to the use of soap. *(See also **Infandous**.)*

Niaiserie. (Nee-<u>ae</u>-zer-ree) **n**. *Foolishness arising from naivety*. As exemplified by investing one's life savings in a Guaranteed Income Fund run by a highly respected member of the peerage.

Nimiety. (Ni-<u>miy</u>-e-tee) **n**. *Excess*. That which can make one feel good on a cold night out, but which can also put one out cold for the night, and possibly for good.

Nippitate. (<u>Ni</u>-pi-taet) **n**. *Good ale*. As distinct from 'real' ale (which, quite frankly, tastes like something excreted by a badger).

Nisus. (<u>Niy</u>-s's) **n**. *An impulse*. The only possible excuse for trying 'real' ale.

Nithing. (<u>Niy</u>-dhing) **n**. *An objectionable wretch*. Specifically, the owner of a pub that sells only 'real' ale.

Nonage. (<u>Noe</u>-nij) **n**. *The state of being under age.*

> '*Offering the nonage gift,' a custom still to be seen in parts of Lincolnshire, involves the administration of 'real' ale (by force if necessary) to those in their nonage who are on the brink of coming of age. The purpose of this curious practice is to induce nausea and vomiting in the young person, and thus prevent their acquiring a taste for 'real' ale when they come of age. Even a casual observer passing through Grantham on a Saturday evening will, however, be led to question the efficacy of the procedure.*
>
> L. Moreton Westlake
> *Traditions of the East Midlands* (2006)

Non-ens. (Non-<u>enz</u>) **n**. *Something that does not exist*. This may also be used to mean a thing that, in a well-ordered universe, *ought* not to exist. Examples are too numerous to list here, but for a start one might mention actors who believe that an ability to learn and repeat words written by somebody else makes them uniquely qualified to pronounce on matters of politics and ethics (or, indeed, on anything else).

Nonillion. (No-<u>ni</u>-ly'n) **n**. *One million to the power of nine, i.e., 1 followed by 54 zeroes.* This word, although strictly not ever actually lost, was used for the first time in June 2008 by the President of the World Bank, when he made reference to the exchange rate of the Zimbabwean dollar against the Namibian nango nut.

Nowed. (Nowd) **a**. *Knotted.* A term used in relation to a state of complex, tight and sometimes inextricable contortion in a length of pliable material. Alternatively, it may be used when expressing the view that the attainment of such a state is, in the case of an individual person or group of persons (e.g., members of the European Commission), cordially recommended. *(See also **Apoious, Aporrhœa, Eident** and **Larrup**.)*

Nowy. (<u>Noe</u>-ee) **a**. *Possessing a curved protuberance near the middle point.* A technical term used by anatomists in relation to aficionados of nippitate *(q.v.)*.

Nubilate. (<u>Nyoo</u>-bi-laet) **vt**. *To make something unclear (literally: to cloud an issue).* Nubilation is the stock-in-trade of those who, whilst knowing little or nothing, wish to appear to know much, an end usually achieved by employing long words where short ones would have sufficed. Thus, a graphologist, having examined a sample of handwriting and given an appraisal of the writer's personality, when asked to explain his reasoning, might refer to 'highly complex psychographological considerations.' The short (and honest) version would be 'I made it up.'

Nugacity. (Nyoo-ga-si-tee) **n**. *A trifling idea*. A useful word to describe any idea which, though presented as novel and profound, is neither of these. Perpetrators of modern art, for example, may explain that the idea behind their latest exhibit is to make people think about how nasty war is, or how pollution will probably make things rather tiresome for us all. It makes one wonder why we never had these insights into the human condition before we went to Tate Modern and saw that tin of baked beans skewered on an umbrella.

Nullifidian. (Nu-lee-fi-dee-'n) **n**. *One who has no religious beliefs*. Also useful to mean someone who has no interest in taking out an insurance policy.

Nundination. (Nun-di-nae-sh'n) **n**. *Buying and selling*. Specifically, the activities associated with running a gift shop in a convent.

Nyctitropism. (Nik-ti-troe-pizm) **n**. *Turning at night*. A phenomenon worth studying in detail when it involves the nocturnal turning of leaves on a plant, but which is best avoided when the turning is into something with hair on its palms.

Nympholept. (Nim-foe-lept) **n**. *One who entertains a passionate enthusiasm for an unattainable goal*. Usually applied to a starlet whose dreams of appearing in a film with George Clooney are brought no nearer despite her increasingly frequent, and increasingly energetic, appearances on the casting couch, though the term may also be used to mean a lifelong supporter of Crewe Alexandra.

Nytel. (<u>Niy</u>-t'l) **vt**. *To busy one's self with trivial matters.*

> *The bureaucrat*
> *Was sleek and fat.*
> *He wore a suit*
> *With a silk cravat,*
> *And issued edicts —*
> *Just like that.*
>
> *He worked all day*
> *In a busy way,*
> *A sign on his door*
> *Said 'Go away.*
> *Signed, Merton Haddock,*
> *MBA.'*
>
> *And everyone thought*
> *That his work was vital —*
> *But all that he did all day was*
> *Nytel.*

O

Obelize. (<u>O</u>-be-liyz) **vt**. *To condemn as corrupt*. Also, in the case of a junior functionary who's seen the version of the accounts the auditors didn't get their hands on, 'to find yourself fired from employment in Brussels.'

Obliquate. (<u>O</u>-bli-kwaet) **vt**. *To twist*. What a cabinet minister subsequently does to the claret-assisted words he used the previous evening, not having realized, until the morning papers arrived, that one of the dinner-party guests was a journalist. *(See also **Babblative**).*

Oblocution. (O-blo-<u>kyoo</u>-sh'n) **n**. *Slander*. A very expensive truth.

Obreption. (Ob-<u>rep</u>-sh'n) **n**. *The acquisition of something by deceit*. As may now be used of someone who wins a parliamentary seat in a constituency where a substantial portion of the ballot consists of postal votes. *(See also **Fleer**.)*

Obsecrate. (<u>Ob</u>-si-kraet) **vi/vt**. *To beg*. To seek payment for sitting down and doing nothing useful. Alternatively, 'to be a member of a quango.'

Obstringe. (Ob-<u>strinj</u>) **vt**. *To put someone under an obligation.* This may be achieved by acts of kindness and generosity, though a legally binding contract is surer, and blackmail is quicker.

Obtenebrate. (Ob-<u>ten</u>-i-braet) **vt**. *To overshadow*. What great men do to those of lesser stature, and what the lowliest bush in the graveyard does to the greatest of men.

Obtestation. (Ob-te-<u>stae</u>-sh'n) **n**. *Beseeching by invoking the name of a deity*. As in 'For God's sake don't mention religion.'

Od. (Od) **n**. *A force supposed to pervade the material universe, and by virtue of which animate beings are affected by inanimate objects, such as crystals and magnets.* May be used when referring to the force that causes money to move along the lines of cosmo-psychic energy which converge upon the pockets of practitioners of complementary therapies. *(See also **Ampullosity**, **Latrant**, **Morology** and **Nagualism**.)*

Olid. (<u>O</u>-lid) **a**. *Having an intensely unpleasant smell*. As of a rat, when a Budget speech mentions a reduction in taxation.

Omophagist. (Oe-<u>mo</u>-fa-jist) **n**. *One who eats raw flesh*. In India, a man with a death wish; in a television chef's house, a man with a highly developed sense of self-preservation. *(See also* **Impone, Incocted** *and* **Keck**.*)*

Onomatomancy. (O-noe-<u>ma</u>-toe-man-see) **n**. *Divination based upon names*. For example, predicting that a boy called d'Arcy Bumstrode is going to have quite a rough time at school.

Oppignorate. (O-<u>pig</u>-n'r-raet) **vt**. *To pawn*. The Sunday tabloids have recently reported that, as a way of paying off a student loan, oppignorating one's personal possessions is second only in popularity to selling one's body.

Oppilate. (<u>O</u>-pi-laet) **vt**. *To obstruct*. A word carrying conno- tations of pleasure combined with both vindictiveness and self-righteousness, as, for example, when used in the context of those given to cycling two abreast, and to no particular purpose, around narrow country lanes with the rest of the cycling club.

Optation. (Op-<u>tae</u>-sh'n) **n**. *The expression of a wish*. For example, that Volvos were fitted with rocket-propelled grenade launchers for emergency use in country lanes.

Opuscule. (Oe-<u>pu</u>-skyool) **n**. *An exceptionally short literary work*. What the novels of Henry James would mercifully have been if brother William had kept that 'stream of conscious-ness' idea to himself.

Orismology. (O-riz-<u>mol</u>-o-jee) **n**. *The explanation of technical terms*. Derived from *orismos* (the sensation of falling), oris-mology was originally 'the study of sinking feelings.' It appears to have been in the early 1990s when the word also acquired the meaning noted above; it was around that time that electronic equipment began to appear on the British market accompanied by manuals noting that the instructions for using the equipment had been 'transdicted from Chinese tongue-producing voice-sounds, with helpings of from-English-to-Chinese fits-in-trousers word-meaning book.'

Ort. (Ort) **n**. *Leftovers*. Those bits of a country that still function after politicians have instituted what they always refer to as 'reforms.'

Orthoepy. (Or-<u>thoe</u>-e-pee) **n**. *Correct pronunciation*. What a person thinks he is using when, unaware of the principle that a gentleman does not need to prove he has had a classical education, he pronounces 'minutiae' as 'my nooty eye' in-stead of 'minooshee.'

Oryctology. (O-rik-<u>to</u>-lo-jee) **n**. *The study of fossils*. An alter-native name for gerontology.

Oscitation. (Os-i-<u>tae</u>-sh'n) **n**. *Drowsy inattentiveness*. That which permits a lecturer to determine the average number of dental fillings per student.

Osse. (Os) **n**. *A good-luck wish*. Particularly one which is expressed when placing a bet at Aintree.

Ostent. (<u>O</u>-stent) **n**. *A portent*. A sign which tells an astrologer that there will continue to be a sucker born every minute.

Overslaugh. (<u>Oe</u>-ver-slor) **vt**. *To pass over one person in favour of another*. Also, when used intransitively, means 'to behave in a manner revealing that one feels threatened by competence or by independence of thought.'

Overslip. (Oe-ver-<u>slip</u>) **vi**. *To pass unnoticed*. A term useful in the publishing industry when referring to books that fail to be received with the critical acclaim that the publisher feels they deserve: as happened, for example, with the three-volume essay *What I Did in the Holidays* by James Joyce.

P

Pabulous. (<u>Pa</u>-byoo-l's) **a**. *Providing food.*

> *No more the fields of golden corn,*
> *That smiled on sunny country lanes;*
> *No more the happy, bustling farms,*
> *Or fertile England's pabulous plains.*
>
> *Long gone the herds of gentle cows;*
> *No raspberries on clinging canes.*
> *Our agriculture's now replaced*
> *By airports crammed with pabulous planes.*

*(See also **Crool** and **Estrepement**.)*

Palillogy. (Pa-<u>li</u>-lo-jee) **n**. *Emphasis achieved by the repetition of a word or phrase.* A useful dramatic device, though it can soon become tiresome if overworked:

LADY HAMTHORPE [*delighted at the compliment*]: My dear Lord Crieff, you are too, too kind.

LORD CRIEFF: Not at all, Lady Hamthorpe; not at all. I always mean what I say.

LADY HAMTHORPE: Oh, I do hope not, Lord Crieff,
I really do. It does so take the element of surprise
out of a conversation, and certainly – most certainly
– out of a social relationship!

LORD CRIEFF [*smiling*]: Oh, it should not do that, dear
Lady Hamthorpe, most definitely it should not – since
I very, very seldom say what I mean.

Henry Wykes Wilberforce
A Most Presentable Lady (1887)

Palingenesy. (Pa-lin-<u>jen</u>-i-see) **n**. *Resurrection*. According to
Professor Karl Bantrup (*Biblical Etymology*, 1938), 'pa'lin'
and 'genez,' the colloquial Aramaic words for 'to strike' and
'forehead,' respectively, combine in the word 'pa'lingenez,'
which means 'a flash of understanding.' Its change of use
may be traced to its appearance in the 1633 Weidenheim
version of St John's gospel, where it was applied to Mary
Magdalene's realization that a person she hadn't recognized
(and who, if she had been asked to hazard a guess, she would
have said was probably the gardener) was actually someone
with whom she had been closely acquainted for years.

Palter. (<u>Pol</u>-ter) **vi**. *To play fast and loose*. As, for example, to
play chess with a hyperactive trollop.

Pancratic. (Pan-<u>kra</u>-tik) **a**. *Of perfect mental discipline*. May
be applied specifically to cooks who adhere rigidly to the
smallest detail of every recipe.

Pandurate. (<u>Pan</u>-dyur-r't) **a**. *Fiddle-shaped*. Useful for describing those who consume the food prepared by non-pancratic cooks who deviate from recipes by doubling up on the sugar.

Paper-stainer. (<u>Pae</u>-per-<u>stae</u>-ner) **n**. *An inferior author*. Though not necessarily one who hasn't produced a string of international bestsellers. *(See also **Gabber**.)*

Paralogism. (Pa-<u>ra</u>-lo-ji-z'm) **n**. *Faulty reasoning*. For example, the following syllogism is faulty:

> *She is a woman.*
> *She is a bad driver.*
> *Therefore, all bad drivers are women.*

The correct conclusion should, of course, be:

> *Therefore, all women are bad drivers.*

Paraphonesis. (Pa-ra-foe-<u>nee</u>-sis) **n**. *A wandering of the mind*. A philosopher in a desert.

Parget. (<u>Par</u>-jet) **vt**. *To whitewash*. When used by a chairman of a government-instituted inquiry, it means 'to come to a carefully reasoned conclusion, following a prolonged, detailed and objective examination of all the evidence.' *(See also **Zetetic**.)*

Parœmia. (Pa-<u>ree</u>-mee-a) **n**. *A proverb*. As, for example, that quoted most often in China:

> *An African dictator in the palm of the hand is worth two who speak approvingly of George W. Bush.*

Parrhesia. (Pa-<u>ree</u>-zha) **n**. *Freedom of speech*. In Great Britain you must not confuse the freedom of speech (reflecting your fundamental human right to utter words) with the freedom to say (reflecting what other people regard as their fundamental human right to tell you what those words can or cannot be).

Parvanimity. (Par-va-<u>ni</u>-mi-tee) **n**. *Small-mindedness*. A technical term in biology, used to describe the mental processes of an amœba or of (what on the evolutionary scale amounts to much the same thing) a religious zealot.

Pash. (Pash) **vt**. *To shatter into bits*. What the Astronomer-Poet recognized as the prerequisite to remoulding this sorry scheme of things entire.

Pasilaly. (<u>Pa</u>-si-lae-lee) **n**. *A universal spoken language*. Another word for English.

> *Although the inhabitants of European countries, in order to irritate the British, sometimes pretend not to understand English, their bluff can easily be called. When speaking to Italians, add an 'o' or an 'a' to every word (add two or three of each, if it proves absolutely necessary); with Spaniards mince*

about and lisp appallingly; and with the French raise your shoulders to touch your ears and hold out your hands, palms up, to the side. Germans give in as soon as you jab a stiffened right arm at their forehead. The Dutch and the Danes lack the imagination to hide the fact that they speak English perfectly. The Swedes, Norwegians and Finns speak English far better than the English do, and like to show off about it — so give them a wide berth. No-one speaks to the Belgians anyway.

Algernon Poge-Withers

Brits Versus the Rest (1975)

Patefy. (Pa̱-ti-fiy) **vt**. *To disclose*. Or, when speaking of a politician's memoirs, 'to nubilate' *(q.v.)*. *(See also* **Hight**.)

Patible. (Pa̱-ti-b'l) **a**. *Capable of being endured*. A quality the BBC believes to be possessed by the Eurovision Song Contest, despite evidence that during the time that the programme is being televised there is a significant rise in the suicide rate in all countries except Belgium.

Patrociny. (Pa-tro̱-si-nee) **n**. *Patronage*. A system which ensures that those of an independent turn of mind are kept firmly in economic circumstances which preclude their disturbing the smooth workings of the status quo.

Pavid. (Pa̱-vid) **a**. *Timorous*. As a wee, sleeket, cowran beastie.

Paynim. (Pae̱-nim) **n**. *A heathen*. Paynims come in many guises, but none more florid than the English visitor to France who stays only at *chambres d'hôtes* owned by English people, so as to avoid speaking French or eating French food.

Pea-chick. (<u>Pee</u>-chik) **n**. *A vain young person.*

> *This strange term was invented in 1985 at the 15th Congress of Neurology held in Leipzig. Professor Heinz Grimsch presented a nuclear magnetic resonance image of the extraordinarily small brain of Helga Schlüpp, a German supermodel. When Grimsch commented that the young lady's cerebral matter was about the size of a chick-pea, Walter H. Hood, an American neurologist, suggested that Fräulein Schlüpp might therefore accurately be described as a 'chick-pea-chick,' an inelegant term which has subsequently been shortened, on æsthetic grounds, to 'pea-chick.'*
>
> Haruhito Kobimura
Medical Terms in Everyday Language (2007)

Peccant. (<u>Pe</u>-k'nt) **a**. *Sinning*. A few years ago, a well-known Sunday tabloid newspaper attracted universal admiration for its report of a murder trial in which it referred to the defendant, a hen-pecked man who had poisoned his wife (described as 'utterly ghastly' by all who knew her), as being 'more pecked against than peccant.'

Pedantocracy. (Pe-dan-<u>to</u>-kra-see) **n**. *A system of government in which pedants rule.* No country has, to date, ever adopted such a system, because those who aspire to rule are generally incapable of the precision of thought that defines the true pedant. It is, however, the only form of government under which there would be the slightest chance of ensuring universal literacy, numeracy and good manners.

Peirastic. (Piy-<u>ra</u>-stik) **a**. *Experimental*. If this term occurs in an invitation to a concert, theatrical production or art exhibition, one should always seriously consider suicide as an alternative.

Peltry. (<u>Pel</u>-tree) **n**. *Rubbish*. A word derived from the surname of Vernon Peltry, a Cornish artist whose entire lifetime output of over four thousand oil paintings was publicly burnt by his widow three days after his death in 1951, as 'an appropriate judgement of their artistic merit.' *(See also* **Cultch** *and* **Mullock**.*)*

Peract. (Per-<u>akt</u>) **vi/vt**. *To perform*. What actors and aquatic mammals do to obtain food.

Perissology. (Pe-ri-<u>so</u>-lo-jee) **n**. *The use of more words than necessary*. May also be used to mean 'publication' when speaking of Sunday newspapers. *(See also* **Macrology**.*)*

Perpension. (Per-<u>pen</u>-sh'n) **n**. *Careful consideration*.

> *Politicians have always realised that it is dangerous to encourage those they are governing to engage in perpension of any matter upon which legislation is intended, because too clear an appreciation of the complexity of a situation*

inevitably exposes as inadequate the simplistic solutions that politicians always propose, thereby destroying the already fragile illusion that the country is governed by people who know what they are doing.

Keiran T. Harwick
Politics: The Art of Distraction (2003)

Perpession. (Per-<u>pe</u>-sh'n) **n**. *The endurance of suffering.* Also, that personality trait common to those who, of their own volition and undrugged, drink creosote or watch an Andrew Lloyd Webber musical.

Philoprogenitive. (Fiy-loe-proe-<u>je</u>-ni-tiv) **a**. *Showing a marked tendency to procreative activity.* Alternatively, descriptive of an industrious pastry cook.

Physeter. (Fiy-<u>see</u>-ter) **n**. *A large blowing whale.* Huge, blubber-encased, gas-emitting mammal. Also, a technical term increasingly useful to surgeons.

Piacle. (<u>Piy</u>-a-k'l) **n**. *Atonement.* A generic term for truly awful films.

Piceous. (<u>Piy</u>-see-'s). **a**. *Inflammable.* In 1896, the Reverend Walton Fairclough wrote in his diary of 'my dear wife's piceous culinary skills,' which led to her serving carbon, in a multiplicity of forms, for dinner.

Pickthank. (<u>Pik</u>-thank) **n**. *A sycophant.*

RIP

SIR WILFRED PICKTHANK

(1922–2002)

HERE LIES SIR WILFRED PICKTHANK,

REMEMBERED FOR THE PRAISE

HE LAVISHED ON SUPERIORS

THROUGHOUT HIS EARTHLY DAYS.

OF FAULTS HE SAW IN OTHERS,

SIR WILF WAS NEVER CRITICAL,

HIS KNIGHTHOOD GAINED

BY WORDS WELL AIMED,

AND FLATTERY POLITICAL.

BUT IF HE'S NOW IN HELL,

IT WOULDN'T BE SO ODD,

FOR, WHILE ALIVE, HE NEVER THOUGHT

OF LICKING UP TO GOD.

Pinguescence. (Pin-<u>gwe</u>-s'ns) **n**. *The condition of becoming fat.* In the UK, this has now replaced what used to be called adolescence.

Plenist (<u>Plee</u>-nist) **n**. *One who holds that no vacuum exists.* A person who has never spoken to a British prime minister in the last decade, and has never met anyone who has.

Plerophory. (Pleer-<u>ro</u>-for-ree) **n**. *Absolute certainty*.

FILIGROU: In all the years I spent in Heidelberg, I craved but one thing. I cared not that my food was meagre, my clothes ragged and my lodgings filthy, but only that that which I sought could – would – ultimately be mine.

MEPHISTOPHELES [*smiling*]: Then you are a fortunate man, Filigrou, to have lacked only a single thing.

FILIGROU: Yes, but what a thing!

MEPHISTOPHELES: A thing for the possession of which you would give…?

FILIGROU: Anything. Everything.

MEPHISTOPHELES: Ah!

FILIGROU: Can you help me? *Will* you help one who has laboured through the cold, dark hours in the dust-laden library of the University of Heidelberg?

MEPHISTOPHELES: Assuredly.

FILIGROU: Then do so, I beg you. Do so.

MEPHISTOPHELES: First seal the bargain. [*Filigrou cuts his hand and allows the blood to fall upon the hem of Mephistopheles's gown*]. So! Now, Filigrou of Heidelberg – you may put your request.

FILIGROU: I desire plerophory – absolute certainty. [*Urgently*] Give that to me, so that I may be at peace. Give me plerophory.

MEPHISTOPHELES: Then hear me. There is but one absolute certainty.

FILIGROU: And that…?

MEPHISTOPHELES: And that is the absolute certainty
    that man will never believe there to be no absolute
    certainty. [*smiling*] Are you now at peace, Filigrou?
FILIGROU [*despairing*]: I do not know.
MEPHISTOPHELES [*now grown cold and aloof*]: Are you
    certain of that?

Wilhelm Schäuenhaft

Dr Filigrou of Heidelberg (1932)

Poietic. (Poy-e-tik) **a**. *Creative*. Percival Howard Grange, one
of the lesser-known Lakes poets, was frequently disparaging
of the work of William Wordsworth, which he described in
his poem 'Grieving for Grasmere' as:

> *Less poetic than pathetic;*
> *Less poietic than emetic.*

Politure. (Po-li-tyur) **n**. *Elegance of manners*. In 1955, Freda
Olwinksi, who specialized in the supply of suitable pets to
the very wealthy, provided the opera singer Dame Myra
Hopple with a mature parrot. Unfortunately, the parrot's
previous owner, a peer of the realm, had been inclined to
use uncouth language in private, and several of the choicer
terms had become incorporated into the bird's vocabulary. Mrs Olwinski, mortified, accepted the return of the
parrot, which she assiduously retrained, succeeding eventually in eliminating its bad language and replacing it with
graceful phrases, such as 'Good morning, ma'am,' and 'I
trust that you are well today.' The Olwinski technique of

'parrot culture' attained fame virtually overnight, and Mrs Olwinski's services were much sought after. What became known popularly as 'polly culture' subsequently entered the language as 'policulture' (later contacted to 'politure') when the methods applied by Mrs Olwinski to parrots became widely adopted by parents of badly spoken children.

Pollinctor. (Po-<u>link</u>-tor) **n**. *A person responsible for preparing a body for cremation*. The post, and thus the title, of Public Pollinctor was discontinued in 1993 after Mordred Llandrenny, an Assistant Pollinctor in Abergavenny, was dismissed for malpractice. Although full details of the case were never made public, it is believed that fireworks (including several rockets) were involved.

Polyhistor. (Po-li-<u>his</u>-t'r) **n**. *A scholarly man*. A person who, in provincial British universities, is now referred to as 'dead wood.'

Pravity. (<u>Pra</u>-vi-tee) **n**. *Depravity*. But shorter, and probably less fun.

Prepollent. (Pri-<u>po</u>-l'nt) **a**. *Possessing superior power*. A term used in a brief public information film released in 1992 by the Campaign for Environmental Responsibility in an (ineffective) attempt to counteract Red Sea Oil's aggressive advertising campaign for their lead-rich Prepollent Petrol. Media consultants Hudson-Wills Inc. came up with the film's slogan: 'Don't let your car poison the atmosphere with its repellent prepollent propellant,' which was later turned into a successful popular song by Jimmy Heinz.

Prevene. (Pree-<u>veen</u>) **vi**. *To take anticipatory action*. Prevention by prevening is not always possible, because it necessitates prediction. Because no-one has yet determined the genetic risk factors for producing a child that will grow into an executive director of a major bank, we cannot, at present, prevene by instituting a socially desirable programme of preventive sterilization or targeted compulsory contraception.

Prosopolepsy. (Pro-<u>soe</u>-po-lep-see) **n**. *Respect for persons*. In 2006, the UK government tried to introduce measures to promote the idea of 'respect,' in the hope that by so doing they would have some effect on the increasing level of violence in our society. The initiative was doomed to failure, being based upon a fundamental misunderstanding.

> *Respect must be earned, but in today's world seldom is. To receive courtesy, however, is everyone's right; and to offer it, everyone's duty. There are those (and, I regret to say, far too many) whom I do not respect, though I pray that, should I chance to encounter any of them, I would always treat each with courtesy.*
>
> Philip Malpass
> *On Courtesy* (1927)

Get that right and the rest follows. *(See also* **Bonair** *and* **Comity**.*)*

Protervity. (Pro-<u>ter</u>-vi-tee) **n**. *Waywardness*. Whatever the arguments may be for the role of natural selection in determining man's anatomy and physiology, it is undoubtedly protervity that has been, and remains, the true driving force of human social evolution.

Protreptic. (Proe-<u>trep</u>-tik) **a**. *Didactic*. Protreptic forms of instruction are regarded by modern educationalists as being too simple, clear and direct, and also too closely linked to the imparting of factual and conceptual knowledge, to be of the slightest use in the classroom.

Psychagogue. (<u>Siy</u>-ka-gog) **n**. *A raiser of spirits*. A publican.

Pudicity. (Pyoo-<u>di</u>-si-tee) **n**. *Modesty*.

> *'I am so fair!' the maiden cried.*
> *'The sweetest girl you'll ever see;*
> *My smile is like the risen sun;*
> *My dress sense is exemplary!*
> *A single fault is all I have —*
> *A leaning to pudicity.'*

Q

Quag. (Kwag) **vt**. *To shake something soft*. What a dinner guest does in order to indicate his refusal of a glass of decent claret and, in so doing (though he may not realize it), his desire not to be invited back.

Quaquaversal. (Kwae-kwa-<u>ver</u>-s'l) **a**. *Pointing in all directions*. A Latin-based word that aptly describes the behaviour of a modern Roman if, throwing caution to the wind, you ask him the way to the Forum.

Questrist. (<u>Kwes</u>-trist) **n**. *One who searches for someone*. Another Latin-based word, this applies specifically to a person who is looking for a friend who, three days ago, asked an Italian the way to the Forum, and hasn't been seen since.

Quiddle. (<u>Kwi</u>-d'l) **n**. *A fastidious person*. In Sheffield, this would be applied to a hostess who, being concerned to maintain the pristine whiteness of the tablecloth throughout a dinner party, is careful to lick the top of the wine bottle after filling each guest's glass.

Quillet. (<u>Kwi</u>-lit) **n**. *A subtle distinction*. A knighthood awarded to someone for being nice.

Quilting. (<u>Kwil</u>-ting). **n**. *A flogging*.

> *Sir Mallory Quilter (Bart.) (1525–1588), commander of Her Majesty's galleon* The Silver Horse, *was a stern disciplinarian. Any sailor who departed even slightly from the rigid code of conduct that Quilter laid down, was publicly flogged. With advances in cultural enlightenment, 'Quilting' as the practice of public flogging became widely known, died out over three hundred years ago.*
>
> The New Universal Encyclopaedia
> Third Edition (1926)

Quinkle. (<u>Kwin</u>-k'l). **vt**. *To extinguish (a light — or, indeed, hope).*

> *Quinkle, quinkle, little Earth,*
> *How I wonder what you're worth.*
> *You are just a ball of dust*
> *Now your banks have all gone bust.*
> *Quinkle, quinkle, little Earth,*
> *Sweet effay is all you're worth.*

R

Ragman. (R̲a̲g̲-man) **n**. *The devil*. A name also given to the person who took the decision that Marks & Spencer's off-the-peg trousers could have leg lengths of 31 or 33, but not 32 inches.

Rakeshame. (R̲a̲e̲k̲-shaem) **n**. *A dissolute person*. Specifically, one who drinks secretively in the potting shed.

Randan. (R̲a̲n̲-dan) **n**. *Disorderly conduct*. A word derived from the name of Sir Archibald Randan who, in 1924, whilst conducting the Birmingham Symphony Orchestra in a public performance of Beethoven's Fifth, abruptly terminated the performance and ran amuck through the orchestra, finally using his baton to stab the second violinist, for whom he had conceived an irrational hatred.

Rantipole. (R̲a̲n̲-tee-poel) **n**. *A reckless person*. Nowadays a term that would be applied specifically to a solitary East European who shouts abuse at a group of fifty or so Manchester United supporters.

Rathe. (Raedh) **adv**. *Without delay*. A concept no longer recognized within the UK postal system following the decision to abandon the first postal delivery of the day, leaving only the second.

Ravin. (R̲a̲-vin) **n**. *Gluttony*. In 1926, neo-Freudian psychiatrist Dr Mordecai Ravin treated melancholia by prescribing a series of thirty gastronomically diverse meals at the elegant Viennese restaurant Das Goldene Vlies, where it was usually exceptionally difficult to make a reservation (the restaurant being a popular venue for the social élite of Vienna). Remarkably, Ravin's patients were always accorded well-placed tables. Ravin was widely credited with making depressive illness not only socially acceptable but actually fashionable, and even the revelation, in 1931, that he was co-owner of Das Goldene Vlies failed to dampen the enthusiasm of the pre-war Viennese for what had become known as 'ravinous therapy.' It was Heinrich Wolff, whose own psychoanalytic practice had suffered as a result of Ravin's popularity, who made 'ravin' synonymous with 'gluttony' by reporting in the *European Journal of Melancholia* (1933) that all Ravin's patients rapidly became massively obese.

Rebarbative. (Ree-b̲a̲r̲-ba-tiv) **a**. *Repellent*. Useful for describing someone with a particularly unpleasant beard.

Receptary. (Ree-s̲e̲p̲-tar-ree) **n**. *A self-evident truth*. A term used in philosophy, and which has recently been explained in the following way:

A receptary is a statement of belief, which, though shown to be simplistic (if not, indeed, downright wrong), is nevertheless perpetuated and vigorously defended. An example of a receptary is the assertion that counselling does more good than harm. The challenge is not, however, to demonstrate the simplistic or erroneous nature of receptaries, but first of all to understand how and why they attain such status, and then to decide who gains what from their doing so.

Aldous Ryle

Aspects of Modern Belief (2006)

Reckling. (Rek-ling) **n**. *The smallest in the family*. When this is your friends' youngest (Octavius, or Jocelyn, or some such name) who tears the title pages out of your collection of modern first editions, while his parents explain to you approvingly that he likes to investigate the properties of materials, it also carries the meaning 'one who doesn't realise how close he is to being blue-lighted to A&E,' and may also be used adjectivally to mean 'short-lived.'

Reclude. (Ree-klood) **vt**. *To shut someone off from something*. As, for example, quite accidentally to lock a reckling *(q.v.)* in the cellar.

Recrement. (Re-kri-m'nt) **n**. *The useless part of anything*. Now appropriated as a technical term by managers of NHS hospitals, who use it to encompass all patients and medical staff, without whom the system would work perfectly.

Redargution. (Re-dar-<u>gyoo</u>-sh'n) **n**. *Refutation*.

> *There once was a bishop called Berkeley*
> *Who had an odd thought, and said, darkly,*
> *'This chair and that ball*
> *Are sense data, that's all:*
> *Nonexistent – to put it quite starkly.'*

> *Though many have rushed to dispute it,*
> *And crashing in flames tried to shoot it,*
> *A mere scepticism*
> *Towards solipsism*
> *Just isn't enough to refute it.*

Refocillation. (Ree-fo-si-<u>lae</u>-sh'n) **n**. *Reanimation*. Specifically, bringing a dead judge back from death to senility.

Refricate. (<u>Re</u>-fri-kaet) **vt**. *To stimulate the memory*. In 2001, the Swiss pharmaceutical company Löwenstoff Pharma AG announced the synthesis of beta-fumarosine, a memory-stimulating compound. *The European Financial Record* reported the subsequent rise in the value of the company's shares from 265 to a record 8,992 Swiss francs in only two days, under the headline 'Francs for the Memory.'

Regrator. (Ri-<u>grae</u>-t'r) **n**. *A middleman*. Someone who stands between you and something you'd like to get your hands on. A term that has been applied in recent times to the British prime minister's bodyguard.

Reif. (Reef) **n**. *Robbery*. A term once used in the UK to describe the practice of selling Australian wine for more than £2 a bottle, but which may now be applied to selling it at any price.

Relict. (Ree-<u>likt</u>) **a**. *Abandoned*. As, for example, to find one's self alone on a desert island, or in Retford.

Reluct. (Ri-<u>lukt</u>) **vi**. *To object*. Or, when used in the context of a local authority's decision to sell off playing fields to a property developer, can mean 'to excrete into the wind.'

Remord. (Ree-<u>mord</u>) **vi**. *To examine one's conscience in a spirit of penitence*. It is a curious fact that those political leaders who are most voluble on the subject of their own Christian beliefs seem not to be concerned that remording is fundamental to the doctrine they profess to follow. But perhaps one should not really be too surprised, since other Christian precepts, such as those about not killing, loving one's enemies, forgiveness, and the rejection of worldly wealth, also don't appear to cause them much in the way of sleepless nights. *(See also **Fardel**.)*

Renable. (<u>Re</u>-na-b'l) **a**. *Elegant of speech*. Listening to recordings of Noël Coward, one could almost believe that to be renable might have something to do with possessing clarity of thought, until one hears the equally elegant words of some of our political leaders.

Reptation. (Rep-<u>tae</u>-sh'n) **n**. *The act of creeping or crawling*. Also a useful climbing technique. *(See also **Hawse** and **Pickthank**.)*

Rescribe. (Ree-<u>skriyb</u>) **vt**. *To respond in writing*. At one time, one used to receive courteously phrased handwritten letters from children thanking one for a birthday or Christmas gift; nowadays, however, the communication often takes the form of a computer-printed note:

> *Dear* _____,
> *Thank you for your* _____ *which I*
> *liked very much.*
> *Yours* _____

Clearly, the parents of those sending these abominations have not the slightest idea of the effect they have upon the recipient.

Retund. (Ree-<u>tund</u>) **vt**. *To drive back*. What the British did to Julius Caesar on two occasions (despite the spin he put on it in his *War Commentaries*). One can't help feeling, though, that if he'd had a decent car he'd have been only too glad to drive himself back to Gaul after having had a quick look around Slough.

Rindle. (<u>Rin</u>-d'l) **n**. *A small stream*. A rindle, though arising from a spring of crystal clarity, and being in the early part of its course transparent and pure, soon becomes murky as it is sullied by the unsavoury detritus it collects on its continuing path, and ends its life sluggish, opaque and full of rubbish. The term can also be used to refer to someone at the commencement of a promising career in politics.

Roborant. (Roe-bor-r'nt) **n**. *A restorative, invigorating substance.* That which gives you life — especially if it's found in your baggage at Bangkok airport.

S

Sade. (Saed) **vt**. *To make someone weary*. This may be done in an hour or two by putting a person through an extended period of intense physical exercise, or in a matter of minutes by telling them about your last holiday, particularly if it was in Estonia.

Saginate. (<u>Sa</u>-ji-naet) **vt**. *To fatten up an animal*. As used in Middlesbrough, it means 'to take your girlfriend out to dinner.'

Salsuginous. (Sal-<u>syoo</u>-ji-n's) **a**. *Impregnated with salt*. Used by the gastronomes of Rochdale instead of 'toothsome.'

Salvatory. (<u>Sal</u>-va-tor-ree) **n**. *A place of safe storage*. A word of curiously mutable meaning. Thus, when one is speaking of the safe storage of sensitive personal information by any government department, 'salvatory' can mean 'a lay-by on the A6,' 'a plastic carrier bag in the bottom of the wardrobe,' 'the back seat of an unlocked car,' 'local authority tip' or 'skip,' according to the government department concerned. *(See also* **Dern** *and* **Derve**.*)*

Sapid. (<u>Sa</u>-pid) **a**. *Possessing a pleasant taste*. A term that, were it to be reintroduced, would be likely to find wide usage – except, of course, in Barnsley.

Sawney. (<u>Sor</u>-nee) **a**. *Foolishly sentimental*. May be used to describe, for example, someone who cannot bear to throw out a pullover knitted in green and yellow wool with a pink rabbit motif on the front, because it was a Christmas present from a close relative.

Scelerate. (<u>Sel</u>-er-r't) **a**. *Apallingly villainous*. Useful when referring to any close relative with even a passing interest in knitting.

Sciolist. (<u>Siy</u>-o-list) **n**. *A person who conceitedly professes knowledge, whilst possessing but a smattering, if any*. The term can refer to more or less anyone putting forward their views on the radio or television after first being introduced as 'an expert,' but it is particularly applicable to those individuals described as 'psychologists.' How one longs for some courageous programme presenter to say, after thanking a psychologist for his or her views, 'And you will, of course, be putting onto our programme's website full details of all the empirical evidence to back up what you've just said, together with a methodological critique of any studies you quote. Won't you?'

Scrat. (Skrat) **n**. *An hermaphrodite*. This is believed to be the only word to have entered English from the language of the A'hutu, a tribe of pygmies living in the Amazon basin. Viscount Marmaduke Fitzwalter, a 19th-century explorer, recorded that the A'hutu numbered no more than fifty, of which all but four were men; when, through an interpreter, he enquired about the imbalance between the sexes, and whether this might not cause some degree of unrest amongst the male members of the tribe, the pygmies did not seem to understand his concern.

> *They merely smiled broadly and flapped their hands in the air, as is their way when expressing amusement. I noticed that the word 'scrat' was mentioned many times, but when I enquired of Kri'ig, my interpreter, what this meant, he claimed ignorance of the term, though I detected that the true reason was a reticence to translate it for me. I pressed him upon the point, however, and when I finally offered him my silver cigar case, which he had long coveted, he explained, albeit with some reluctance, that 'scrat' was the A'hutu word for 'having it both ways.'*

> Viscount Fitzwalter
> *Pygmy Hunter* (1886)

Scrobiculate. (Skroe-<u>bi</u>-kyoo-l't) **a**. *Characterized by a large number of shallow depressions.*

> *The term 'scrobiculate' was introduced into psychiatry by Adolf Freud (Sigmund Freud's nephew) during the time that he worked in Stoke-on-Trent in the early 1930s. Adolf rejected the conventional diagnostic labels of medical psychiatry, which he replaced with his own mixture of abstruse and colloquial terminology. Thus he recorded an unusually high proportion*

of the population of Stoke-on-Trent as being 'scrobiculate' (drifting in and out of minor depressions), and therefore falling into his broader diagnostic category of 'miserable buggers.'

Fulton J. Heaversham
Adolf Freud: A Biography (1989)

Secern. (Si-<u>sern</u>) **vt**. *To make a mental distinction*. To offer a prize to the one who has caught most fairies in a jam jar.

Seely. (<u>See</u>-lee) **a**. *Blissfully happy*.

THE FABLE

Johnny and Jeanie were living in clover.
They had a nice house with a garden (near Dover),
A wonderful marriage, successful careers,
No mortgage, no debts, no commitments, no fears.
When Jeanie got pregnant their joy was complete:
They'd soon hear the patter of dear little feet.
Their life to that point had been blissfully happy,
But neither had reckoned with changing a nappy.
'Good God!' said poor Johnny. 'Do babies do that?
I'm sure, if we'd known, we'd have chosen a cat.'
Post-partum depression, and bitter remorse
Led soon to a very expensive divorce.

THE MORAL

Beware of contentment and feeling too seely:
Remember that life's never perfect — not really.

Septentrional. (Sep-<u>ten</u>-tree-o-n'l) **a**. *Northern*. A term that may be applied accurately only to those who regard Keswick as being somewhere in the Midlands.

Sequacity. (Se-<u>kwa</u>-si-tee) **n**. *A readiness to follow*. A condition which can be induced by an extraordinarily wide variety of circumstances, such as: (1) you've had a bad day's fishing in Galilee, when along comes someone suggesting a change of catch; (2) the floor is tilted at forty-five degrees, and you see a sign saying 'This way to the lifeboats'; or (3) you're in the middle of a Meryl Streep film, and you hear someone say 'This is crap. I'm off.'

Shebeen. (Shee-<u>been</u>). **n**. *A low inn*. Any establishment where the wine list is not dominated by the wines of France.

Shent. (Shent) **a**. *Disgraced*. What it was presumably intended that a person should be when made the subject of an Antisocial Behaviour Order (ASBO). However, amongst those who believe that reading involves listening to the teeny-weeny sounds that paper makes, 'shent' is synonymous with 'regarded with admiration.'

Shog. (Shog) **vi**. *To ride bumpily*.

> *Come, friendly cars! Cut through the field*
> *That once its golden corn would yield;*
> *Smash through the hedge and charge four-wheeled.*
> *Across it shog.*

We get our crops from Chile now,
And have no need for hoe or plough.
You hardly ever see a cow;
So bring your smog.

Churn up our fertile English soil,
With hand-brake spins; and drip your oil.
There's nothing left for you to spoil.
Turn it to bog.

They've cleared the barns of all the cats,
And from the farmhouse chased the bats.
They've turned it into luxury flats,
And shot the dog.

No ducks or chickens to be fed;
No pigs; no goats. The farmer's dead:
He put a shotgun to his head —
No more to slog.

Come, friendly cars! Knock down the gate.
Deep in the field are seeds that wait;
Make sure that they don't germinate —
Above them shog.

Siccity. (<u>Si</u>-ki-tee) **n**. *Dryness*. The Siccity Scale is used in evaluating the dryness of jokes. It is not to be confused with the Sickity Scale, which relates only to jokes about physical disability or terminal illness.

Sigillate. (<u>Si</u>-ji-laet) **vt**. *To seal up*. It was from this word that the name of the Sigillatory movement was derived. The Sigillators held the view that if every building of government, including the Palace of Westminster, were sealed, there would be no discernible consequences for the life of the country. An unsuccessful attempt was made in 1978 by two leading members of the group, Major Patrick W. Birkett and Miss Marcia Knotte, to seal the Home Office and Treasury buildings with fast-setting cement applied by pressure pump to ground-floor doors and windows.

Simkin. (<u>Sim</u>-kin) **n**. *Champagne*. A word now heard only when someone is calling for the fifth or sixth bottle.

Skelder. (<u>Skel</u>-der) **vt**. *To cheat*. Based upon the name of Arnold Skelder, a well-known jockey in the 1950s who only narrowly missed being Champion Jockey in each of three successive flat-racing seasons. In 1959, Skelder was reprimanded by the Jockey Club for having deliberately come last in a race when riding Desert Cloud, then favourite for the Derby (which was to be run the following month), in an attempt to lengthen the odds on the horse. The phrase 'skelder the odds,' meaning 'come well down the field,' is used in racing stables throughout the land.

Skelp. (Skelp) **n**. *A slap*.

> *The etymology of 'skelp' is exceptionally tortuous. In the mid-1950s, Lady Gloria Skelp, youngest daughter of the Marquis*

of Pendlebridge, became notorious for her disorderly parties — or 'skelps' as they became known. Soon, the term 'skelper' was applied to any female invited to a 'skelp' and in the popular media a 'skelper' became equated with a 'slapper.' Over time, 'skelp,' through the process known as 'linguistic contiguity,' became synonymous with 'slap.'

Jeremy Froggart
Slanguage: Origins of Colloquialisms (2000)

Skirr. (Sker) **vi**. *To flee*. Originally used in the sense of making a judicious withdrawal from a skelp *(q.v.)* before it turned nasty, but later applied in the more general sense of making a rapid exit from anywhere — as in the widely used saying 'to skirr the skelp,' meaning 'to skip the country' or 'to do a bunk.'

Slabby. (<u>Sla</u>-bee) **a**. *Sloppy and viscous*.

> *She was a most revolting wench,*
> *In manner coarse and crabby,*
> *She bought her clothes from jumble sales,*
> *And looked ill-dressed and shabby.*
> *She lunched till three at KFC —*
> *No wonder she was flabby.*
> *But worst of all, as I recall,*
> *Her kisses were … well … slabby.*

Slat. (Slat) **vi**. *To flap vigorously*. A word that describes perfectly the action that follows the ten-second period of total immobility after one has just opened an income tax bill in which the sum owing has two commas in it.

Sliddery. (<u>Sli</u>-der-ree) **a**. *Slippery*. As applied to the slope on which teenage dyslexics stand when they first start drinking alcopops.

Slive. (Sliyv) **vi**. *To loiter*. To be used exclusively of those who hang around Graceland.

Sloomy. (<u>Sloo</u>-mee) **a**. *Spiritless*. A dingy pub for depressed Saudis.

Slowback. (<u>Sloe</u>-bak) **n**. *A sluggard*. One who makes a study of the ways of ants.

Slub. (Slub) **vt**. *To plaster with mud*. A nice short word that in the newpaper industry is sometimes used to mean 'to publish.' *(See also **Daggle** and **Lutarious**.)*

Smutch. (Smuch) **n**. *A moral stain*. Moral stains in others are particularly visible to those whose regular attendance at church ensures their own freedom from such blemishes. One cannot, however, help wondering how the morally pure know with such certainty what it is they are looking for.

Snell. (Snel) **a**. *Clever*. A term of unreserved admiration that may be applied to seals that can hold balls on their nose, and men who can hold their nose on their balls.

Snip-snap. (<u>Snip</u>-snap) **vi**. *To engage in witty repartee.* As two guests might do at a dinner party whilst some of the other diners reflect upon how the discussants might react to the snipping of vital body parts, and the rest weigh up the chances of successfully using a defence of temporary insanity to get away with snapping the snip-snappers' spines.

Snudge. (Snuj) **n**. *A sponging fellow.* A hard-up window-cleaner.

Sortilege. (<u>Sor</u>-ti-lij) **n**. *Witchcraft.* Auguste Périleau, Minister of Waterways under President de Gaulle, had a deep loathing of committee meetings, and accordingly perfected a manner of slipping out of them in such a way that his absence always passed unnoticed for at least an hour. He subsequently made a small fortune by publishing a book, *Une Sortie Légère* (1979), describing his technique. Soon, whole committees found their numbers were reduced by two-thirds within ten minutes of starting business, without anyone being seen to leave the room. As a consequence, 'sortie légère' quickly became synonymous with 'magic' or even 'witchcraft,' and it was in this latter sense that it passed, in its contracted and anglicised form, into the English language. Curiously, no English person has ever managed to make Périleau's technique work – at least, not that anyone has noticed.

Soum. (Soom) **n**. *Pasturage needed to support one cow.* Once an important concept in mediæval agriculture, this is now used as a legal term in determining financial settlements in divorce proceedings.

Spang. (Spang) **n**. *A strong kick*. Also, the name of a new form of rapid-action psychotherapy for the treatment of work-related stress.

Spatchcock. (<u>Spach</u>-kok) **vt**. *To insert*. Used recently by disgraced celebrity chef Len Loomis in his book *Culinary Techniques Your Mother Didn't Know* (2007). The book became a bestseller after Loomis appeared on a live cookery programme on BBC television and demonstrated what he termed the 'spatchcock method' of stuffing a duck. Loomis, who was subsequently banned from appearing on all British television channels, received a suspended sentence.

Spatiate. (<u>Spae</u>-shee-aet) **vi**. *To ramble*. A word which would serve perfectly, for those who know their geography, to mean 'to weave one's way between the Aberlour, Cardhu, Dufftown, Glendronach, Glenfarclas, Glenfiddich and Glen Grant distilleries.'

Streel. (Streel) **vi**. *To trail on the ground*. Even though the fingernails of most humans safely clear the tarmac, I have reached the conclusion, after watching CCTV footage of Saturday-night scenes in most British city centres, that maybe knuckle-to-ground distance is not the best measure of evolutionary advancement. Indeed, it sometimes takes the crystal accent of Miss Joanna Lumley to convince me that evolution is still working.

Surquidry. (<u>Ser</u>-kwi-dree) **n**. *Arrogance*. Derived from the name of Sir Quinian Dree, who refused to bow to Queen Victoria and Prince Albert, both of whom he regarded as riff-raff.

Synonymist. (Si-<u>no</u>-ni-mist) **n**. *One who makes lists of synonyms.* May also be used of any individual who shows a lack of enthusiasm for leaving the house.

T

Tabefy. (<u>Ta</u>-bee-fiy) **vi**. *To waste away*. First used in 1973 by Dr Enrico Guiducci, in his report of a near-disastrous experiment he had conducted in which, over a nine-week period, he had fed ten people nothing but cat food.

Tartarean. (Tar-<u>tair</u>-ree-'n) **a**. *Infernal*.

WHY THE WORLD
WENT TO HELL

The golden lamp had been dug up,
In studies archæological,
Then taken to an Expert for
Its placement chronological.

'Now, I must first,' the Expert said,
'Clean off the grime and grit.'
And taking up a duster he
Began to polish it.

Just then an old and bearded man,
Of practice pedagogical,
Recalled a book that he had read
On matters mythological.

'That object is a magic lamp,'
He thought, 'or I'm a weevil!
With, deep within its golden bowl,
A genie – plotting evil.'

'Don't rub that lamp. It isn't safe!'
Cried out the antiquarian.
Too late! The genie, now released,
Commenced his work tartarean.

Tenebricose. (Te-ne-bri-koez) **a**. *Gloomy*. A term that has been relatively little used in the UK since the invention of the electric filament light bulb, but which is expected to show a resurgence in popularity when it becomes mandatory to use only low-energy light bulbs. The revitalised term will also carry the associated meanings of being rendered blind by the ultraviolet light low-energy bulbs emit, and poisoned by the mercury released when they're broken.

Tephromancy. (Te-froe-man-see) **n**. *Divination by the examination of ashes*. A ritual practised in Australia, but virtually unknown in England.

Terebrant. (<u>Te</u>-ri-br'nt) **a**. *Belonging to the class of boring insects*. Also, a generic term for the kind of man who sits next to you at dinner and delights you with an account of his collection of Victorian clothes pegs, or enthrals you by explaining at length how Princess Diana faked her own death and is now living with a plumber in Penge.

Tergiversation. (Ter-ji-ver-<u>sae</u>-sh'n) **n**. *The abandonment of a cause*. Often thought of as the action of a rogue, but usually that of someone who has suddenly got smart.

Theroid. (<u>Theer</u>-royd) **a**. *Possessing a bestial nature*. A medical condition in which the sufferer feels an overwhelming compulsion to interfere with all warm-blooded animals and most cold-blooded ones, and which appears to be related to erratic functioning of an endocrine gland in the neck.

Thirl. (Therl) **vt**. *To pierce*. May also be used as a noun when speaking of the sound made when a man who's paid good money to have a chunk of metal stuck through his tongue explains that he did it to impress a 'girl.'

Thole. (Thoel) **vt**. *To tolerate*. What an oppressed populace does until it dawns upon them just how considerably they outnumber a dictator and his thugs.

Tirrit. (<u>Ti</u>-rit) **n**. *A sudden onset of fear*. What a dictator experiences immediately before making a quick dash to the nearest helicopter, having just realised that the crowd outside the presidential palace won't thole *(q.v.)* his rotten regime any longer.

Tittup. (<u>Ti</u>-tup) **vi**. *To walk in an affected, bouncy, up-and-down manner*. Particularly apposite for referring to those who model clothes on the catwalk, and even more so when speaking of contestants in the Miss World pageant.

Tony. (<u>Toe</u>-nee) **n**. *A foolish person*. No kidding. You just couldn't make it up.

Tostication. (To-sti-<u>kae</u>-sh'n) **n**. *Distraction*. It has long been the policy of the Downing Street press office to 'bury bad news' – i.e., to wait for a major world event to dominate the headlines, and hence distract the public, before revealing yet another government debacle. Keith Spoon, Conservative MP for Lytham South, was reprimanded by the Speaker of the House of Commons for referring to the government's Chief Press Officer as 'that well-known tosticator,' though the Speaker, to his credit, having had the precise meaning of the word explained to him, subsequently apologized to Mr Spoon for the inappropriate reprimand. *(See also* **Intumulate**.*)*

Triplicity. (Tri-<u>pli</u>-si-tee) **n**. *Threefold character*. A politician's version of duplicity. *(See also* **Monocephalous**.*)*

Tritical. (<u>Tri</u>-ti-k'l) **a**. *Of an inconsequential nature*. Applicable specifically to the writings of literary critics.

Tuftaffeta. (Tuf-<u>ta</u>-fe-ta) **a**. *Dressed luxuriously*. Also, the soubriquet awarded by the *New York Times* to Albert Finglethorpe, an eighteen-stone professional wrestler from Arkansas with a penchant, when relaxing at home, for wearing frilly frocks.

Turdiform. (<u>Ter</u>-di-form) **a**. *In the form of a thrush*. Small and brown, and flies away chirping when the sample jar is opened.

Tutty. (<u>Tu</u>-tee). **n**. *A posy*.

> *When Miss Geraldine Hogge took over the long-established* Henderson's Florists *in the High Street, her first act was to change its name to* The Tutty Shop, *which she felt would be particularly eye-catching. She was certainly proved right about that, but not in quite the way she expected! At a talk given by Miss Hogge on Wednesday to the Business Women's Section of the Bybridge Chamber of Commerce, she revealed that ever since the new name had appeared on the sign above the shop's window she had been plagued with literally hundreds of embarrassing queries from men who had misread it.*
>
> Report in the *Bybridge Record*
> 7 June 2002

U

Ugglesome. (<u>U</u>-g'l-s'm) **a**. *Horrible*. The converse of 'ogle-some.'

Ultracrepidarian. (Ul-tra-kre-pi-<u>dair</u>-ree-'n) **n**. *An ignorant critic*. As, for example: a literary critic who has never written a novel; a film critic who has neither acted in nor directed a film; a music critic who hasn't been a member of an orchestra; or an art critic, whatever he or she may or may not have done.

Ultroneous. (Ul-<u>troe</u>-nee-'s) **a**. *Voluntary*. The concept of voluntary action, the product of free will, has always fascinated philosophers who, presumably of their own free will, have tackled the issue in various ways.

> SOCRATES: Tell me, my dear Meno – what was it that made you come to see me today?
> MENO: I wished to speak with you.
> SOCRATES: Ah! So your decision to visit me was entirely voluntary?
> MENO: Yes, Socrates, I believe so.

SOCRATES: And do the Gods know of your action in
  coming here?

MENO: Yes, that I also believe.

SOCRATES: Why do you believe it, Meno?

MENO: Surely it is obvious. The Gods are omniscient.

SOCRATES: Being omniscient, the Gods must know
  not only what you have done and what you are now
  doing, but also what you will do in the future.

MENO: That is so. Because they are omniscient, the Gods
  must know all these things.

SOCRATES: But, my dear Meno, how could they know
  yesterday that you would visit me today?

MENO: They could only have known that, Socrates, if my
  decision had been preordained.

SOCRATES: Then, if preordained, it could not have been
  voluntary.

MENO: But I do assure you, Socrates, that it was
  voluntary.

SOCRATES: Then the Gods could not have known that
  you would take that decision.

MENO: If it had been voluntary, then that is true – they
  could not have known.

SOCRATES: In which case, Meno, you cannot say that the
  Gods are omniscient.

MENO: So it follows, does it not, Socrates, that if, as I
  truly believe, I have free will and can act voluntarily,
  the Gods are not omniscient; but if, as I also truly
  believe, the Gods are omniscient, none of my actions
  can be voluntary?

SOCRATES: That does seem to follow.

MENO: How may this paradox be resolved?

SOCRATES: It may be resolved only if either the Gods or you do not exist, Meno. Which do you think the more likely?

Plato

The Precepts (circa 362 BC)

*(See also **Autexousy**.)*

Underfong. (<u>Un</u>-der-fong) **vt**. *To seduce.*

> *Some way out of Barndale there lies a tract of high ground, rather too rocky and heather-covered to be of any agricultural use apart from the grazing of a few sheep and the occasional goat. Near the midpoint of The Furzle, as this place is called, stands a curious tree, of a type that I have seen nowhere else in the British Isles. Some thirty feet tall, and with wide, spreading branches, it bears large silver-green leaves and in autumn is covered with red flowers possessing a heavy, sweet scent. This, I was told, is known, for reasons that have long passed out of local memory, as the Fong Tree. In times gone by, the gently sloping hillock upon which it stands was a favourite trysting place for lovers, and even now in Barndale a wooing consummated out of wedlock is referred to as having been achieved 'under the Fong.' Hence 'to underfong' has come to mean 'to seduce one who is not entirely unwilling.'*

Charles W. Opple

Terms of Seduction (1929)

Unhele. (Un-<u>heel</u>) **vt**. *To discover*. Ever since some idiot tried to blow up an airliner by setting fire to his shoes with a match, airport security has become obsessed with looking for high explosives in footwear. It therefore occurred to me that 'unhele' might be reintroduced to describe the discovery of Semtex in a pair of brogues, but as a terrorist would have to be really stupid to pack the stuff into a place that was bound to be searched, I rejected the idea. But then again, you have to be pretty dim to think that blowing yourself to smithereens is likely to be seen by anyone as a persuasive argument for the soundness of your beliefs, so maybe I was on to something after all.

Unscience. (Un-<u>siy</u>-'ns) **n**. *Ignorance*. Unscience is the name assigned by science teachers to the combination of chemistry, physics and biology that is now being taught as a single subject in UK schools.

Ustulation. (U-styoo-<u>lae</u>-sh'n) **n**. *The act of burning*. Specifically applicable to that culinary process which, when done to beef, makes the French recoil and the English salivate.

V

Vappa. (<u>Va</u>-pa) **n**. *Sour wine*. The inevitable consequence of sour grapes.

Vare. (Var) **n**. *A rod*. A technical term applied by aviarists to a pole serving as a perch.

Vaticinate. (Va-<u>ti</u>-si-naet) **vt**. *To predict*. Specifically, to predict the likely lifespan of any Pope who asks to see the financial records. *(See also **Birkie**.)*

Vegete. (Vi-<u>jeet</u>) **a**. *Healthy*. A word which is used to describe: (1) breakfast cereals that are high in fibre and low in fat, but contain enough sugar to kill a zebra; (2) patients who begin 'I've had this problem for about thirty years, doctor'; and (3) people who use an online symptom checklist and diagnose themselves as dying of cancer.

Velleity. (Ve-<u>lee</u>-i-tee *or* Ve-<u>lae</u>-i-tee) **n**. *The condition of wishing for something without being inclined to do anything about it*. The mental state of around two-thirds of the British electorate.

Vellicate. (Ve-li-kaet) **vt**. *To titillate.* A term introduced in 1950 by Dr Ralph Jordan, in a talk given to the Société Historique de Provence and entitled 'Vellication – or titillation on vellum: fifteenth-century pornographic manuscripts discovered in the vaults of the Abbaye de St Pierre, Haut Lubain.'

Venefice. (Ve-nee-fis) **n**. *Sorcery using potions with magical properties.* An alternative name for homœopathy. *(See also **Illation**.)*

Ventifact. (Ven-ti-fakt) **n**. *An object, the shape of which has been determined by the way the wind blows.* Also, the opinion which a politician holds on any matter which has the potential to affect the voting behaviour of the electorate.

Versute. (Ver-syoot) **a**. *Crafty.* A term that can be applied to a bearded sculptor.

Vesania. (Ve-sae-nya) **n**. *Madness.*

> *One thought it schizophrenia;*
> *Another called it mania;*
> *A third resolved the matter when*
> *He diagnosed vesania.*

Vitiosity. (Vi-shee-o-si-tee) **n**. *A vice.* Sir James Crabbe, speaking in 1653 at his trial on a charge of voyeurism (he had admitted spying upon a group of ladies who were bathing *au naturel* in a quiet stretch of the upper Thames), is reported to have said:

If curiosity be deemed a vitiosity, then look now upon the most vitious of men.

Roland Sanderson

Famous Seventeenth-Century Trials (2001)

The case was dismissed.

Vorticist. (<u>Vor</u>-ti-sist) **n**. *An adherent of a school of art which attempted to combine Cubism, Futurism and Expressionism.* The original name of this early 20th century art movement was 'Synthetism.' It was in 1929 that the new term 'Vorticism' became attached to it following publication of an article in *Art and Artists Today* by Howard Thropper, art critic and prolific writer on art history. Thropper expressed the view that 'In their attempt to reconcile several fundamentally irreconcilable approaches to modern art, the Synthetists have found themselves swept up into a swirling mass of confused ideas, struggling ever harder in their doomed desperation to find a way out of their predicament – only to be sucked finally into the vortex of their own artistic fundament.' The word 'vorticist' may thus usefully be applied today to anyone who, by being too clever by half, digs a hole from which there is no escape.

W

Wamble. (<u>Wom</u>-b'l) **vi**. *To feel nauseous*. Particularly on Wimbledon Common. *(See also* **Howish***.)*

Wanhope. (<u>Won</u>-hoep) **n**. *Despair*.

ROSE: How can you say such things, Albert? I do believe you enjoy being cruel to me.

ALBERT [*aghast*]: Oh, Rosie!

ROSE: It's true. I can't help how I feel. Every word you speak seems like a poisoned shaft. What future is there for me now? I feel only wanhope.

ALBERT [*surprisingly cheerful*]: Well, at least that's better than no hope at all.

ROSE [*sobbing, and running from the room, her hand clutching her forehead*]: Oh, you beast! You beast! How could you?

Edward Charles Bligh
The Unsuitable Suitor (1911)

Washbrew. (<u>Wosh</u>-broo) **n**. *A jelly-like substance that the Scots produce by the prolonged boiling of oatmeal in water. The best,* and also a sufficient, argument for granting Scottish independence.

Wherret. (<u>Hwe</u>-r't) **n**. *A slap*. Also, a technique developed in Sweden, which is a useful adjunct to spang *(q.v.)* therapy.

Whillywha. (<u>Hwi</u>-lee-hwar) **vt**. *To flatter*. Useful primarily in the context of sexual prowess.

Wisht. (Wisht) **a**. *Dismal*. From 'Wyschte,' the Anglo-Saxon name for Crewe.

Wistly. (<u>Wist</u>-lee) **adv**. *With close attention*. At one time, this applied to the comportment of pupils in the classroom, but the term is now useful only in describing behaviour in the vicinity of anything with a screen.

Wite. (Wyt) **n**. *The torment of hell*. According to documents released from the BBC archives, it was originally intended that *The Archers* should be called *The Wites*. Those who remember the feeling of numbness that gripped them when they switched on the radio on Whit Monday, 1950, to get their regular dose of *Dick Barton – Special Agent*, only to hear some drivel about 'an everyday story of country folk,' will wonder what idiot decided that *The Wites* was not entirely appropriate.

Wittol. (<u>Wi</u>-t'l) **n**. *One who tolerates his wife's infidelity*. May be used in the sense of 'someone who knows exactly what he's up to,' if his wife is one of the huge, lumbering, wobbling, triple-chinned creatures that try to pass themselves off as females these days.

Wone. (Woen) **n**. *Opinion.*

> *That which fills any space not occupied by knowledge.*
> Sir Patrick Goodman-Pryce
> *Collected Correspondence* (1941)

Woodman. (<u>Wud</u>-m'n) **n**. *A maniac.* One of Adolf Freud's psychiatric diagnostic categories, an interest in axes coming high on the list of diagnostic features. *(See **Scrobiculate** for information about Adolf Freud.)*

Wray. (Rae) **vt**. *To denounce.*

> *The Vicar of Wray was a fine, moral man.*
> *Who thought up an excellent, idiot-proof plan*
> *To rid his good parish of women and men*
> *Of whom it was said 'They've been at it again.'*
> *He said, 'From the pulpit, those rogues I'll denounce,*
> *Unless they see fit their romance to renounce.'*
> *But little they cared for the things he would say,*
> *For there's something, you know, in the air around Wray.*
> *Yes, something that lovers detect on the wind.*
> *And so did the Vicar; and that's why he sinned –*
> *And then from the pulpit his shame he confessed.*
> *'Alas,' said the people, 'we thought he knew best.*

> *But now it's quite clear he's no better than us.*
> *We really can't see why he kicked up that fuss!'*
> *The Vicar, denounced, left the very next day,*
> *And that was the end of the Vicar of Wray.*

Wye. *(Wiy)* **n**. *A soldier.*

> *A warrior, a fighting man,*
> *He's strong of arm and clear of eye;*
> *He looks upon the Afghan plain —*
> *This British wye.*
>
> *A roadside bomb of crude design —*
> *Though this may be the way he'll die,*
> *He seeks in vain an answer to*
> *The question 'Why?'*

X

Xantippe. (Zan-<u>ti</u>-pee) **n**. *A shrewish wife.* Though not the wife of a shrewd man.

Xenelasy. (Ze-<u>nee</u>-la-si) **n**. *A means of driving away foreigners.* Though some countries have to spend a large proportion of their gross domestic product on keeping out foreigners, there are other states, such as Belgium, that are perfectly capable of achieving the same result without any expense at all.

Xenogenic. (Ze-noe-<u>je</u>-nik) **a**. *Unlike the parent.* A term that may be applied more generally to someone who has discovered how to avoid the inevitable.

Xenomancy. (<u>Ze</u>-noe-man-see) **n**. *Divination based upon the arrival of strangers.* When the strangers arrive in the early hours and take out the front door with a battering ram, it's safe to predict that the only way you're going to have any free time in the future is by grabbing the bag containing the unedited version of the company accounts, the passport with your photograph but somebody else's name, several dozen wads of large-denomination banknotes, and the one-way ticket to Bolivia.

Xerothermic. (Zeer-roe-<u>ther</u>-mik) **a**. *Dry and hot*. The climate of Alice Springs, Phoenix, Riyadh, and Hell.

Xylophone. (<u>Ziy</u>-loe-foen) **n**. *An instrument by means of which sounds may be produced by the striking of flat pieces of wood of different lengths*. Although the word itself (literally: wood-sound) is well known, and I can therefore lay no claim to having rediscovered it, I include it here because my researches have revealed a hitherto unrecorded use of the word – one, indeed, which may throw new light on its modern application. According to documents recently unearthed by the historian Marcus Kreel, to which I have been given access, the term 'xylophone' was applied in the early 14th century to the scream produced in a prisoner hit with a stick. It appears that screams of different pitches could be produced by varying the length of stick, and that gaolers of a musical disposition found that, by such means, they could elicit a pleasing melody. *(See also **Dretch**.)*

Y

Yaffle. (_Ya_-f'l) **vi**. _To talk indistinctly._

> _Though not a man of intellect,_
> _Or knowledge esoteric,_
> _(And further disadvantaged_
> _By his Christian name of Eric),_
> _He gained the highest pinnacle_
> _Of academic standing –_
> _The Nobel Prize for Cleverness_
> _And Brainwork Most Demanding –_
> _An accolade awarded for_
> _His long and complex lectures,_
> _Which everyone agreed contained_
> _Astonishing conjectures._
> _But that's the way it always is_
> _With learned literati –_
> _They fall hook, line and sinker_
> _For a self-appointed smarty._
> _But not a single one of them_
> _Confessed to being baffled_

> *By Eric's public discourses*
> *(For Eric always yaffled.)*

Yain. (*Y*aen) **vt**. *To meet*. As used in the wartime song 'We'll Yain Each Other Again,' which unaccountably failed to seize the public imagination.

Yaply. (<u>Y</u>a-plee) **adv**. *Nimbly*. A word which would serve perfectly to describe the movements of a small dog in an agility test at Crufts.

Yarely. (<u>Y</u>air-lee) **adv**. *Briskly*. A term which may be re-introduced specifically to describe the manner in which the British government moves to introduce any legislation that looks like being a vote winner. The word could also be used in place of the adverbial phrase 'without bothering (or, more likely, without having the ability) to think it through,' or adjectivally to mean 'half-baked.' *(See also **Accurtation, Agible** and **Gleg**.)*

Yarken. (<u>Y</u>ar-k'n) **vt**. *To prepare*.

> *Then saith the Lord: Harken unto me, and yarken the people*
> *of Gethem for the evil that shall darken their land.*
>
> *Book of Heresh* (vi. 11)

It was thus that the Almighty issued his command to the prophet Heresh, though, for reasons not explained in the Bible, Heresh found himself unable to take it seriously – with predictably dire and bloody consequences for the people of

Gethem and (when the Gethemites found out that Heresh had been too doubled up laughing to pass on the warning) for the prophet himself.

Yaud. (*Y*ord) **n**. *An old mare.*

> *I would recommend Yaud as perfectly acceptable for use by a well-bred gentleman who, wishing to express his disapproval of a lady of his acquaintance, is too refined, and of too considerate a disposition, to refer to her by the epithet that might first spring to mind.*
>
> Lady Hermione Blythe
> *Etiquette for Gentlemen of Sensibility* (1902)

Yclept. (Ee-<u>klept</u>) **a**. *Named.*

> *She looked upon her baby's face,*
> *And thought it beautiful to see.*
> *'Receive, my child,' she softly breathed,*
> *'This name I give to thee.'*
> *The name she gave had come to her*
> *In dreams, when deep she slept;*
> *Her child, whose beauty dimmed the Sun,*
> *Was thus Eclipse yclept.*

Yean. (*Y*een) **vi**. *To give birth.* Also used as an onomatopœic substantive, to describe the sound emitted in a loud, high-pitched and drawn-out manner by those who have been persuaded that the science of anæsthetics should be kept at arm's length from the process of childbirth.

Yeie. (*Y*ae) **vi**. *To cry out*. And particularly to make the sound that enthusiastically greets the arrival of an anæsthetist. *(See* **Yean**.*)*

Yete. (*Y*eet) **vi**. *To confess*. A word which, if revived, could prove useful to the American security services, to be used in the specific sense of 'to say whatever is necessary to switch off the electric current, or to prevent one's head being shoved for the twentieth time into a bucket of cold water.'

Yex. (*Y*eks) **n**. *The hiccups*.

> *There is one, and only one, sure and certain cure for the hiccoughs, and that is for the sufferer to count, very slowly and silently, as follows: 'one yex, two yex, three yex …,' and so on, starting again with 'one yex' if a hiccough should occur. The affliction will disappear within no more than half a minute.*
>
> Daisy Cheswick
> *Uncommon Cures for Common Ailments* (1898)

Ylike. (I-<u>liyk</u>) **vt**. *To please*.

A BIRTHDAY GIFT FROM HARRODS
FOR THE MAN WHO HAS EVERYTHING

The Customer
My husband's birthday is next week,
And I must buy a present.
I trust you can facilitate
My search for something pleasant?

The Assistant

Of course, dear lady, never fear.
Regard our fine emporium!
Delights and wonders here abound
To charm a man's sensorium.

The Customer

I do not doubt it, my good man!
Thus from your stock extensive
I'll choose a gift unusual –
And awfully *expensive.*

The Assistant

A Rolex watch? A vintage car?
There's nothing that a buyer
Can not obtain at Harrods:
Tell me, madam, your desire.

The Customer

I'll buy a Harley-Davidson!
I'm sure a motorbike –
Though surplus to requirements –
Will my husband much ylike.

Younker. (<u>Y</u>un-ker) **n**. *A fashionable fellow*. If reinstated into the language, this would now exclude anyone able to knot a tie. In Grimsby, it would exclude everyone.

Yuke. (**Y**ook) **vi**. *To itch.*

> *Mr Wilfred Plank, 58, of Grundyfield Road, Middlewich, told*
> *the court that for over thirty years he had suffered from a*
> *medical condition known as cat-yuke. Characterized by a*
> *particularly intense irritation and itching of the skin and*
> *nasal passages, this unpleasant affliction was apparently*
> *caused by the presence of cats. Mr Plank added that all known*
> *medications, including powerful antihistamine drugs, had*
> *proved totally ineffective against the ailment. Mr Vernon de*
> *Verney, representing Mr Plank, said that his client had, in*
> *desperation and at considerable personal expense, sought a*
> *private consultation with the eminent German immunologist*
> *Professor Heinrich Grünenberg, and had subsequently followed*
> *the professor's advice to the letter. The court did not, however,*
> *accept Mr Plank's explanation in mitigation of the offence,*
> *and imposed a fine of £350 for keeping a shotgun without a*
> *licence.*
>
>

Nantwich Evening Express
22 March 2006

Z

Zelator. (Ze-la-t'r) **n**. *A passionate supporter*. Originally, a device constructed out of steel and wood, designed by Dr Maurice Kelp in 1896, for the treatment of male impotence, and operating on the cantilever principle. Now, however, used primarily to refer to one who watches *Match of the Day* over his wife's left ear.

Zelotypia. (Ze-loe-ti-pee-a) **n**. *Jealousy*. The desire to possess that which belongs to another but which, once possessed, ceases to be desired.

Zendik. (Zen-dik) **n**. *One who rejects prevailing religious dogma*. If one can believe ecclesiastical gossip, it seems that, amongst those in the know in the UK, this term is often used instead of 'bishop.'

Zetetic. (Ze-te-tik) **n**. *An investigation*.

Sir George Penworthy, MP for Hutton and Borwell, was a great enthusiast for the setting up of 'investigations' whenever the probity of the government's conduct was called into question. He sat on eighteen investigating committees during his parliamentary career, chairing all but two of them. Five of the committees never issued a report, their work terminating unfinished after three or four years, when general elections brought all government activities to an abrupt end. The reports of a further nine investigatory committees were suppressed by the government on national security grounds, though in all cases it was difficult for anyone to imagine what aspects of national security might be involved. The remaining four investigatory committees were unable to reach a conclusion because of lack of information. In one case, all twenty-six people called to appear before the committee shot themselves, drowned, or were killed in a bewildering variety of automobile accidents before they could give evidence. When, shortly after his retirement from the House, Sir George was asked whether the investigations with which he had been involved had been a disappointment to him, in view of their inconclusive outcomes, he replied that each had served perfectly the purpose for which it had been set up.

Carole McGrath

Homo Politicus: Penworthy in Parliament (2002)

(See also **Flam** *and* **Parget**.*)*

Zoilus. (Zoe-i-l's) **n**. *A malignant critic*. A word derived from *Zoilus toxicostylus*, the zoological name for the Korean tapeworm. Like this disagreeable animal and similar life-forms, the human zoilus is incapable of an independent existence. *(See* *also* **Creticism, Dedolent, Tritical** *and* **Ultracrepidarian**.*)*

Zorille. (<u>Zo</u>-ril) **n**. *A skunk-like creature*. Also, a term which, in several African countries, means 'President.'

A Note on Alternative
Lexicology

There will be those who, after reading some or all of the entries in this book, may be moved to challenge my claim to have written a work of lexicography, but I maintain that *lexicography*, properly defined, involves no more than the writing-down of a list of words. What is open to discussion, however, is whether or not I have written a work of *lexicology*.

In any good standard dictionary, each of the words listed (the lexico*graphical* element) is followed by a lexico*logical* examination of its meaning, etymology, grammatical and syntactical form, and both its historical and current usages. Although such detailed information is not provided for every word in the *Reliquary*, I am assured that one test of sound lexicological analysis lies in the confidence with which others are prepared to repeat the information in defence of their use of a word in a particular context. I know of some (intelligent folk all – though I cannot provide character references) who take the *Reliquary* as their ultimate authority on such matters. So I hold it to be a work of lexicology.

Nevertheless, I will concede that this book is best regarded as an example of what has been called *alternative* lexicology, in which words are presented less for narrow and specific linguistic purposes than as springboards for the imagination (thought in zero gravity, or, as others might think in my case, in free fall). It is a concession I make without reluctance, my careful research having revealed a long and fascinating tradition of alternative lexicology to which I am very happy to ally the *Reliquary*.

It is my firm intention to write, one of these days, a scholarly thesis on the history of alternative lexicology, but I hope that, in the meantime, the following highly eclectic survey of some of the more notable examples may serve to whet the reader's appetite.

As far as I am able to determine, it was **Thomas Hensley** who, in 1617, first published what may truly be described as a volume of alternative lexicology. His *Expository Dictionarie of the Englishe Tongue* listed 2,856 words which, according to Hensley, reflected English opinion of those 'scoundrels kept without, by these our guardian seas.' From the relatively restrained comment on the word 'Alerte' ('Thus are men of England made vigilant gainst Spaniard and poison-toad'), the book takes an increasingly vertiginous dive into xenophobic hysteria – the only example I can legally quote here being the rhyming couplet 'The tales of wanderings in Hell/That voyagers through France all tell' (a comment on 'Vagarie').

Hensley's work was widely admired in literary circles, and copies of his little book were still being produced in the early part of the 18th century, coming eventually to the attention of philosopher **Benjamin Hollander**, author of *Discourses on Calvinism* (1708). Hollander's *Lexicon* (1715), embraced the style of Hensley's dictionary, linking every one of 3,023 disparate words to some aspect of Calvinism. The *Lexicon* revealed to everyone (as his earlier work, being impenetrable, had not) Hollander's total and spectacular failure to have grasped as much as a single element of the Calvinist doctrine. Hollander consequently lost the respect of his university colleagues, who henceforth shunned his company, and he died a broken, bewildered and unenlightened man. Even on his deathbed, he continued to insist that two of the Doctrines of Grace (Total Depravity and Limited Atonement) gave the green light to the uninhibited enjoyment of life's pleasures.

The publication, forty years later, of Samuel Johnson's *Dictionary of the English Language* (1755) was overshadowed by the appearance, in the same year, of *A Book of Papish Words* by **John Joseph Helminth**. Each of the 2,604 words in this book triggered vivid and stomach-churning descriptions of acts that Helminth argued should be inflicted upon the person of Pope Benedict XIV (even seemingly innocuous terms such as 'Table,' 'Tree' and 'Crow' stimulated Helminth's imagination in unexpectedly violent ways). When a copy of the book reached Rome, it so distressed Benedict that he took to his bed for four months. In March 1758, Benedict issued a papal bull, *De Pathologia Helminthi*, which denounced Helminth as 'mad, vile and evil,' to which the lexicographer replied simply, 'Apple, hen, goblet and rope – these in whatsoever sequence your Holiness may choose.' Benedict died on 3 May 1758, two days after receiving Helminth's letter.

Alternative lexicology burst upon an unprepared 19th century in the form of *The Meanings and Pronouncings of the English Words* by **Gabriella Moricelli** (1800). Moricelli, a Milanese socialite, nursed intellectual pretensions on a grand scale. Totally unfazed by her lack of any formal education, she published during her lifetime some thirty books and pamphlets on an astonishing variety of subjects, ranging from a detailed description of the Egyptian pyramids (which she had never visited) to an appreciation of the music of Austrian composer Heinz Schmutt (none of whose works she had ever heard). True to form, she produced an extended account of English words even though she did not have the advantage of speaking English, or, indeed, of being acquainted with anyone who did. Choosing English books at random from the extensive library of her uncle, Count Fabiano Moricelli, she selected words which she thought 'bellissime' and guessed at both their meanings and pronunciations. The apparent erudition of Moricelli's book threw startled English academics into confusion, at least three hailing it as a work of genius. A facsimile of the 1800 edition was published in 2001, and a copy sent to the BBC for review; although no review was ever broadcast, the book was widely circulated within the BBC, where it appears to have exerted considerable influence on the corporation's newsreaders.

If the 19th century came in with a lexicological bang, it went out with a glorious whimper. In 1898, **Egbert Greenbough** published an eighteen-page booklet entitled *Essential English*. Greenbough contended that English could be reduced to a small number of words which would suffice to express any idea or to communicate any wish or desire. This notion was a clear forerunner of Basic English, introduced in 1930 by Charles Kay Ogden, but whereas Ogden gave a list of 850 'core words,' Greenbough identified no more than thirty-six. In the final two years of her reign, Queen Victoria enthusiastically embraced

Greenbough's ideas, to the consternation and total confusion of the royal household and the Queen's ministers. On ascending to the throne after his mother's death (her last words being 'bag' and 'ferret,' the only nouns in Greenbough's system), the newly crowned Edward VII ordered all copies of *Essential English* to be tracked down and quietly disposed of.

No alternative lexicological effort worthy of the name was produced in the 20th century, which was, let's face it, a pretty dismal hundred years as far as the English language was concerned. Things are, however, looking up in the present century, with no fewer than six substantial works being published in 2008 alone. I shall review all of these in my forthcoming monograph on the subject, but I cannot end without mentioning the work of **Wilberforce Breem**. In October 2008 Breem's *Ow too Spel Inglish* listed 18,498 words that are regularly misspelt by pupils aged 15 to 18, and the twenty-six words that are not (the latter including most, but by no means all, two- and three-letter words).

So there you have it. Alternative lexicology is a fascinating area of study and I have no doubt that, even as I write, there is a student in one of the newer universities polishing off his doctoral thesis on the subject. When I look back at the wonderful alternative lexicological works that have been published over the centuries, I cannot but find my own contribution relatively insignificant. Still, I rejoice in having succeeded, albeit surreptitiously, in tagging my name onto a list of extraordinary scholars, the complexity of whose mental processes defies analysis.